Retrieval of History from Purāṇic Myths

By the same author

- Chandragupta Maurya - A Gem of Indian History
- Founders of India's Civilizations
- Fundamentals of Hinduism
- India in the Vedic Age
- Prachin Bharat Ka Itihas (Hindi)
- Sahitya Vimarsh (Hindi)
- Vedic Religion and Culture

Retrieval of History from Purāṇic Myths

(Exposure of late Purāṇic myths about some great characters of the earliest Indian history)

P.L. Bhargava

DK PRINTWORLD
Publishers of Indian Traditions

Cataloging in Publication Data — DK
[Courtesy: D.K. Agencies (P) Ltd. <docinfo@dkagencies.com>]

Bhargava, P.L. (Purushottam Lal), 1909-2002.
Retrieval of history from Purāṇic myths.
Includes bibliographical references (p.).
ISBN 13: 9788124607404 (PB)

1. Mythology, Hindu. 2. Puranas — Criticism, interpretation, etc. 3. Vedic literature — History and criticism. I. Title.

ISBN 13: 978-81-246-0740-4 (PB)

First published, 1984
Revised and enlarged edition, 1998
Reissued in paperback in 2014

Printed and published by:
D.K. Printworld (P) Ltd.
Regd. Office : *Vedasri*, F-395, Sudarshan Park
(Metro Station: Ramesh Nagar)
New Delhi – 110 015
Phones : (011) 2545 3975, 2546 6019; *Fax* : 2546 5926
e-mail : indology@dkprintworld.com
Web : www.dkprintworld.com

To
Viśvāmitra
the great Aryan prophet of India who gave us
our most holyprayer,
the Gāyatrī

Preface To The Second Edition

The first edition of this book was published in 1984. Encouraged by the high encomiums received from both the prestigious Indological journals and eminent scholars, I am bringing out the second edition. This is, however, not the only reason for publishing the second edition. A few months back a member of our parliament accused Rāma of banishing his wife Sītā, and nobody rose up to point out the wrongness of his accusation. I have therefore in the second edition put the chapter in which I have shown the incorrectness of this belief first, in violation of chronology, and I hope it will dispel the wrong belief of our people. I must express my deep appreciation of the help given by my son Divakar and my grandson Manjul in typing and preparing the manuscript. My grnddaughter Mudita also helped me in typing a portion of the manuscript.

The second edition of this book is being published by D.K. Printworld of New Delhi. Their efficiency and promptness are truly praiseworthy and mark them out as a publisher with a difference.

Richmond, VA, U.S.A. **P.L.Bhargava**
April 13, 1998

Preface to the First Edition

MYTHOLOGY has been the bane of history as of religion. Great personages of the dim and distant past, who inspired their fellow beings by their sublime thoughts and marvellous deeds, lost their historicity when they were enveloped in myths which tended to grow around their names. It is a difficult task to pick out the grain of history from the husk of myths and it is more difficult to produce conviction even when it is picked out after hard search.

It would be absurd to maintain that no great men were born in India before the time of Buddha. In fact most Indologists regard Sudās, the hero of the battle of ten kings celebrated in the *Ṛgveda*, as a historical figure. If so, the names of other great men mentioned in the *Ṛgveda* and other works belonging to Vedic literature need not be regarded as figments of imagination. The Purāṇas and the epics supply copious information about many of them but this information was more and more mythologized with the passage of time. A collated study of the Vedic and Purāṇic literatures makes it crystal clear that fiction took the place of fact by graded and perceptible stages.

I have chosen eight great men of the earliest period of Indian history to illustrate how mythology eclipsed history. So far as three of these characters viz. Rāma, Vyāsa and Yudhiṣṭhira are concerned only some aspects of their stories have been taken up for discussion. They are in due order the genesis of the first and last books of the *Rāmāyaṇa*, the origin of the Purāṇas and the *Mahābhārata*, and the date of the Kurukṣetra war. In the case of the other five personages their entire available account has been studied. I shall feel rewarded if this study shakes the preconception of many Indologists that the history of India before the age of Buddha is irretrievably lost.

I gratefully acknowledge my debt to a galaxy of Indologists whose works have been of both help and inspiration to me. Even when I sometimes differ with some of them, my indebtedness to them is not diminished.

Jaipur **Purushottam Lal Bhargava**
March 1, 1984

Contents

Preface to the Second Edition vii

Preface to the First Edition ix

Transliteration Chart xiii

1. The Purāṇas and the Rāmāyaṇa 1
2. Did Rāma Banish his Wife Sītā? 25
3. Did Rāma kill Bālin Surreptitiously? 31
4. Was Viśvāmitra the Father of Śakuntalā? 35
5. Did Paraśurāma kill his own Mother? 41
6. Did Bhagīratha bring the Gaṅgā from Heaven? 49
7. Did Kṛṣṇa have a Companion named Rādhā? 55
8. Was Yudhiṣṭhira Crowned King of Hastināpura in 3102 B.C.? 69
9. Was Vyāsa the Author of the Traditional Eighteen Purāṇas? 85
10. Was Vālmīki a Robber in his Youth? 93

Appendix 103

Glossary 129

Bibliography 133

Index 137

Transliteration Chart

The following system of transliteration has been adopted in this book:

अ	आ	इ	ई	उ	ऊ	ऋ	ए	ऐ	ओ	औ	ं	ः
a	ā	i	ī	u	ū	r̥	e	ai	o	au	ṁ	ḥ

क	ख	ग	घ	ङ
ka	kha	ga	gha	ṅa
च	छ	ज	झ	ञ
ca	cha	ja	jha	ña
ट	ठ	ड	ढ	ण
ṭa	ṭha	ḍa	ḍha	ṇa
त	थ	द	ध	न
ta	tha	da	dha	na
प	फ	ब	भ	म
pa	pha	ba	bha	ma

य	र	ल	व
ya	ra	la	va
श	ष	स	ह
śa	ṣa	sa	ha

1

The Purāṇas and the Rāmāyaṇa

THE Purāṇas are one of the most important branches of Sanskrit literature. Yet no other work of Sanskrit litrature is as controversial as the Purāṇas. Their importance lies in the fact that one of the subjects of most of these works is the account of the numerous royal dynasties that ruled in India from the period when the Aryans first settled in this country to the period of the foundation of the Gupta dynasty. But it is precisely this account which has made these works the subject of heated controversy.

Now it has to be admitted that so far as the history of the various kings mentioned in the genealogical accounts of the Purāṇas is concerned, the tendency of these accounts is that the more ancient the king, the more his achievements have been exaggerated and mythologized. This was the reason why in the infancy of Purāṇic studies scholars had come to the conclusion that the Purāṇic accounts are worthless as a source of history. A patient study of these works has, however, made it clear that though the Purāṇic accounts of ancient kings may be and actually are in a great measure untrustworthy, it does not necessarily follow that the names of kings themselves, their order of succession, and their total number are also to be regarded as fictitious and untrustworthy.

Fortunately the Purāṇic genealogies from the time of the birth of the founder of Buddhism onward can be tested by the evidence supplied by the Buddhist and Jain literature, dramas and inscriptions. This test shows that although the Purāṇas have given detailed list of kings of no less than ten dynasties viz. those ruling over Avanti, Magadha, Kosala and Vatsa in the time of Buddha and those of Śiśunāgas, Nandas, Mauryas, Śuṅgas, Kaṇvas and Andhras that succeeded them, the mistakes regarding the names, the order of succession and the regnal years of kings are certainly not many. These three things will now be examined separately.

So far as the names of kings in these ten dynasties are concerned it is a noteworthy fact that whenever the Purāṇas differ from the Buddhist or Jain accounts, the independent evidence of dramas or inscriptions supports the Purāṇas. Thus in the Magadhan dynasty of Buddha's contemporary Bimbisāra, the Purāṇas mention a king called Darśaka whose name is not found in the Buddhist and Jain accounts. The existence of this king is, however, proved by the play named *Svapnavāsavadattam* composed by the ancient poet Bhāsa. Similarly the Purāṇas mention a king named Daśaratha in the Maurya dynasty who is unknown to the Buddhists and the Jains. The existence of this king too has been proved by his inscriptions in the Nāgārjunī hills of Bihar. The only mistake found in the Purāṇas with regard to names is the insertion of the names of Śākya, Śuddhodana, Siddhārtha and Rāhula in the list of Kosala kings as predecessors of Prasenajit. This is a deplorable mistake committed by some late editor perhaps to fill the gap caused by the loss of some names, but a solitary mistake cannot destroy the credibility of the entire Purāṇic lists of kings.

When we examine the order of succession of the kings in the Purāṇic lists of post-Buddha kings, we do find a number of misplacements. As rightly observed by Pargiter in his *Dynasties of the Kali Age*, these misplacements have occurred through the carelessness of the copyists and are mostly to be found only in some of the Purāṇas or in some manuscripts of a particular Purāṇa. Only in two cases — those of the Śiśunāgas and the

Andhras — the misplacements are serious, but the evidence of the Purāṇas themselves as well as of other ancient works makes it easy to correct these misplacements. The case of Śiśunāgas will be fully discussed in chapter 8 of this book. So far as the Andhras are concerned, Dr. Raychaudhuri, in his *Political History of Ancient India*, has convincingly demonstrated that the *Vāyu Purāṇa* list of 19 kings in the dynasty proves that the 11 extra kings found in the *Matsya Purāṇa* belonged to some branch of the Andhras and have been misplaced by the copyist of the *Matsya Purāṇa*. Thus a few misplacements that have occurred in the Purāṇic lists of post-Buddha kings do not at all detract from the value of these lists.

So far as the regnal years of these ten dynasties are concerned, it is clear that while the regnal years are by no means fictitious or imaginary, copyists have in the case of these years also sometimes made mistakes due to confusion between numbers whose names are alike such as *triṁśat* and *viṁśat*, *catvāriṁśat* and *caturviṁśat*, *aṣṭāśīti* and *aṣṭāviṁśati, ṣaṇṇavati* and *ṣaḍviṁśati*. These mistakes are, however, few and far between and can easily be corrected. They too therefore do not diminish the historical value of these Purāṇic lists.

If the Purāṇic genealogies from the time of Buddha onward are almost faultless, the presumption naturally is that the earlier genealogies too are not mere figments of imagination. Mere presumption, however, cannot produce conviction. We have, therefore, to examine them from three angles, viz., as regards the authenticity of the names themselves, as regards the authenticity of their arrangement and as regards the authenticity of their number.

So far as the names of kings in the earlier genealogies are concerned, there are two clear proofs of their authenticity. In the first place a large number of these names occur in the Vedic literature which is quite independent of the Purāṇas. Secondly, even those names which do not occur in the Vedic literature are so archaic that they could not have been coined by the authors of the present Purāṇas in whose time the style of names had completely changed. The numerous variations prove that often the authors of the Purāṇas even failed to write them correctly.

The arrangement of name is a very important matter, for, even if the names are genuine, the genealogies will still be worthless if the arrangement of these names is faulty. The correctness of the arrangement of these names is borne out by the evidence of the *Ṛgveda* and other works of Vedic literature. In the first place whenever kings are mentioned by their patronymics such as Yayāti Nāhuṣa, Marutta Āvikṣita, Māndhātṛ Yauvanāśva, Bharata Dauḥṣanti, Trasadasyu Paurukutsi, Dhṛtarāṣṭra Vaicitravīrya, etc., the Purāṇic lists are corroborated. In the case of the Tṛtsu dynasty, the names of eight generations from Bhṛmyaśva to Somaka occur in the same order in the *Ṛgveda* and other Vedic works as in the Purāṇas. The correctness of the arrangement can also be judged in another way. It is noteworthy that only those kings whose names occur in the early parts of the Purāṇic genealogies are found mentioned in the *Ṛgveda* outside the tenth book, while those kings whose names occur in the latter parts of these genealogies are mentioned only in the tenth book of the *Ṛgveda* or the later Vedic literature, but never in the early part of the *Ṛgveda* consisting of books I to IX. The two most important early dynasties according to the Purāṇas were those founded by Ikṣvāku and Sudyumna respectively. In the former some of the famous early kings were Māndhātṛ, Purukutsa, Trasadasyu and Tryaruṇa who are all mentioned in the *Ṛgveda*. In the latter the earliest kings were Purūravas, Āyu, Nahuṣa and Yayāti who are all mentioned in the *Ṛgveda*. Yayāti had five sons named Yadu, Turvaśa, Druhyu, Anu and Pūru who are all mentioned in the *Ṛgveda*. The most famous of these was Pūru whose early descendants, Bharata, Vidatha and Ajamīḍha are all mentioned in the *Ṛgveda*. Among the successors of Ajamīḍha, the most powerful were the Tṛtsu monarchs, seven of whom are mentioned by name in the *Ṛgveda*. But the names of kings, who, according to the Purāṇas, ruled after that, occur only in the later Vedic literature including the tenth book of the *Ṛgveda*, but never in the bulk of the *Ṛgveda*. Further, it is to be noted that in accordance with the testimony of the Purāṇas, according to which the Vedic canon comprising the four *Saṁhitās* was closed before the Bhārata war, we find that no king of the Purāṇic genealogical lists later than Dhṛtarāṣṭra Vaicitravīrya is mentioned in the Vedic *Saṁhitās*. The *Brāhmaṇas* and Upaniṣads do mention names of some kings who ruled after the Bhārata war such as Janamejaya Pārikṣita of Kuru, Ugrasena Janaka of Videha, Pravāhaṇa Jaivali of Pañcāla and Ajātaśatru of Kāśī, but they too do not mention a single king of the post-Buddha period which again proves the trustworthiness of the arrangement of names in the Purāṇic genealogies. The last but not the least important thing which proves the correctness of the arrangement of names in the Purāṇic genealogies is that of synchornisms. There are numerous synchronisms recorded in the Vedic, Purāṇic and epic literatures which are in consonance with the arrangement of names in the dynastic lists of the Purāṇas.[1] These facts clearly establish the correctness of the arrangement of names in the Purāṇic genealogies.

We now come to the third point, viz., the authenticity of the number of names in the lists. If the names are all correct and the arrangement is also faultless, the implication is that the number of kings is also correct. But luckily another source belonging to the fourth century BC is available to prove the antiquity of the number of kings in the Purāṇic lists. The reference is to Megasthenes, the Greek ambassador at the court of Candragupta Maurya. The Greeks, as is well-known, had the peculiar habit of identifying the heroes and gods of other nations with their own heroes and gods. They identified the Indian hero, Kṛṣṇa with their own Herakles. Similarly identifying the first Indo-Āryan king Manu with the Greek god Dionysus, Megasthenes made the statement that "from the time of Dionysus (Manu) to Sandrakottos (Candragupta Maurya) the Indians counted 153 kings".[2] The actual number of kings who ruled during this period according to the Purāṇas comes to 135. This slight difference is really immaterial and we may well regard the statement of Megasthenes as an additional proof of the correctness of the number of kings in the dynastic lists of the Purāṇas.

Sometime ago Dr. D.C. Sircar in an article entitled "Rājavaṁśa Varṇana of the Purāṇas" publised in *Sri Venkatesvara University Oriental Journal*, Vol. XX, Parts 1 and 2 dated January-December 1977, again cast doubts on the authenticity of Purāṇic genealogies. The arguments advanced by him, however, can hardly bear the test of scrutiny. The discrepancy pointed out by him in the Andhra list of kings has already been explained here as being the result of misplacement of some kings by the copyists of some of the Purāṇas. In any case this discrepancy does not make the genealogical account of the Andhras fake or fictitious. The mistakes in the regnal years of few kings like Nandivardhana, Mahānandin, Mahāpadma and Vindhyaśakti are due to confusion caused by similarity of names of certain numbers and are negligible when we remember that in the case of an overwhelming majority of these kings the regnal years give no room for doubt.

The anachronistic reference to Yavanas, Śakas and Pahlavas in the wars and conquests of the ancient kings Sagara and Bāhu is quoted by Sircar as another proof of the unreliability of Purāṇic genealogies. A scholar like him, however, should have known that the tendency of the later editors of the Purāṇas to exaggerate the achievements of ancient kings is responsible for such statements which do not by any means prove that the names of the kings themselves are mythical or fabricated.

Some of the arguments advanced by Sircar to condemn the Purāṇic genealogies unfortunately show scant regard for facts. It is certainly not the fault of the Purāṇas if some late and ignorant interpolater of the *Rāmāyaṇa* has given a fake pedigree of Rāma which does not agree with the Ikṣvāku genealogy of these works. Further it is most unfair to judge the correctness of the genealogical account of the Purāṇas by applying the cosmological chronology of these works to it. Whatever may be the length of the Vaivasvata Manvantara in the cosmological account of the Purāṇas, it has really nothing to do with the chronology of the kings descended from Vaivasvata Manu.

Dr. Sircar goes on to say that "as the Purāṇas appear to represent Manu and his decendants as Aryans, we have probably to regard them as mythical if we accept the theory of Aryan advent about the middle of the second millennioum BC." It is difficult to understand what it is that compels Sircar to accept the theory of Āryan advent about the middle of the second millennium BC. This theory was propounded by Max Müller who himself regarded this date only as a *terminus ad quem*. Winternitz later gave good reasons for holding that the date of Āryan advent was probably the middle of the third millennium BC. Not a single sound reason has been given up to this day in refutation of the arguments advanced by Winternitz in support of the date proposed by him. One cannot therefore help agreeing with this scholar that it has become a habit with Indologists to say that the Āryans entered India in the middle of the second millennium BC. This habit is unfortunately doing great harm to the study and reconstruction of ancient Indian history.

The most astounding statement of Dr. Sircar is as follows: "It may be noticed that the non-Aryan association of some of the clans is quite pronounced. Thus the story of Yayāti of the lunar race suggests that his favourite son Pūru the progenitor of the Pauravas was born of a non-Aryan princess." It is nothing short of extreme highhandedness to regard the mother of Pūru a non-Āryan princess because her father has been called an *asura, daitya* or *dānava*. As we have shown elsewhere,[3] these words, unlike the word *rākṣasa*, never denoted any non-Āryan tribes. As a matter of fact they have been regularly applied to impious Āryan princes in the Purāṇas. Moreover the very names of the princess and her father, Śarmiṣṭhā and Vṛṣaparvan, are purely Āryan, as distinguished from non-Āryan names like Balbūtha, Dhuni and Cumuri occurring in the *Ṛgveda*. It is impossible to believe that such pure Sanskrit names could be borne by non-Āryans in that early period of Indo-Āryan history.

Dr. Sircar asks us also to note the dark complexion of the Yādava hero Kṛṣṇa. He conveniently forgets the fact that Kṛṣṇa's brother Balarāma is invariably described as white in complexion. Similarly although Rāma is said to have been dark or blue in colour, his brother Lakṣmaṇa is always described as white in complexion. The reason why Rāma and Kṛṣṇa are regarded as dark or blue in colour, while their brothers are described as white is not to be sought in anthropology or history but elsewhere. Since Viṣṇu as the god of sky is conceived as blue, it is his colour which has been transferred to his incarnations Rāma and Kṛṣṇa.

It is thus not unjustified to hold that the Purāṇic genealogies are not the figment of the imagination of an idle priesthood, but are based on reliable ancient tradition. Nevertheless, as will be explained in the ninth chapter of this book, both the contents and the number of the Purāṇas grew in the course of centuries and with this growth some of the famous characters of history recorded in these works suffered most. Eight of such characters have been chosen to show how in the course of centuries their real story was completely transformed in some respect or the other. These characters in chronological order are Viśvāmitra, Paraśurāma, Bhagīratha, Rāma, Vyāsa, Yudhiṣṭhira, Kṛṣṇa and Vālmīki. Deviation from this order has been made in two cases. Rāma, being the most popular of the Indian heroes, the wrong stories prevalent about him have been discussed in the second and third chapters. Here too in violation of chronology, the banishment of Sītā, being the most burning topic of the *Rāmāyaṇa*, has been taken up before the episode of Bālin. Similarly, although from the point of age the order of the three contemporary *Mahābhārata* characters should have been Vyāsa,Yudhiṣṭhira and Kṛṣṇa,it has been reversed keeping in view the incidents of their lives, mentioned in these chapters.

It is important to remember that like the Purāṇas the great epic *Rāmāyaṇa* also, which is the primesource for the story of Rāma, lost its original character as a result of additions and interpolations made into it from time to time. Since Rāma is one of the characters chosen for this book, it is necessary to say a few words about this epic.

The *Rāmāyaṇa* in its present form consists of seven *kāṇḍa*s called *Bālakāṇḍa*, *Ayodhyākāṇḍa*, *Araṇyakāṇḍa*, *Kiṣkindhākāṇḍa*, *Sundarakāṇḍa*,*Yuddhakāṇḍa* and *Uttarakāṇḍa*, respectively. The careful investigations of Professor Jacobi[4] have shown that this noble epic originally consisted of five books only (II-VI). The spuriousness of the last book and a large part of the first book has been proved beyond a shadow of doubt by Professor Jacobi. His arguments may be summarized as follows:

1. The human hero of the genuine *Rāmāyaṇa* has in the first and the last books been deified.
2. In these books alone Vālmīki appears as a contemporary of Rāma.
3. There are two tables of contents in the first book, the former of which occurring in Canto I takes no notice of the first and last books and must therefore have been made before these were added.
4. The language and style of these two books is inferior to those of the remaining books.
5. Indra is the highest god in the genuine *Rāmāyaṇa* as against the first and last books where Viṣṇu has attained greater importance.
6. In these books alone the thread of narrative is frequently

interrupted by numerous myths and legends of the type occurring in the Purāṇas and the *Mahābhārata*.

7. The spuriousness of the last book is indubitably proved by the fact that the *Rāmāyaṇa* has been concluded at the end of the sixth book.

8. So far as the first book is concerned it is certain that, some parts of it are genuine and must have been brought here from the *Ayodhyākāṇḍa* when the latter became book II of the *Rāmāyaṇa*. For example the fifth Canto of book I, omitting the first four verses, certainly formed the commencement of the original poem.[5]

The internal evidence of the *Rāmāyaṇa* thus makes it clear that the original *Rāmāyaṇa* consisted of only five books though it should be remembered that some cantos and verses have been interpolated even in the genuine books of the *Rāmāyaṇa,* as we have it today.

Jacobi's arguments though convincing are limited only to the internal evidence of the *Rāmāyaṇa*. It is remarkable that several external pieces of evidence, not mentioned by him, confirm most of what he said on the basis of the internal evidence of Vālmīki's poem. Rāma's story as borrowed from Vālmīki is found with all its important details in seven Purāṇas, viz., *Kūrma*, *Brahma*, *Garuḍa*, *Viṣṇu*, *Agni*, *Bhāgavata* and *Padma* and also in the *Harivaṁśa* and the *Mahābhārata*.[6] These works clearly show the gradual growth of the story of Rāma and wonderfully confirm the conclusions of Jacobi with regard to the *Rāmāyaṇa*.

We shall first take up book I of the *Rāmāyaṇa* and see what light these works throw on the growth of its contents. The oldest account of the early life of Rāma forming the subject-matter of book I of the *Rāmāyaṇa* is found in the *Kūrma Purāṇa*,[7] which gives the following information:

> Daśaratha, son of Aja, had four sons named Rāma, Bharata, Lakṣmaṇa and Śatrughna who were all powerful like Indra and Viṣṇu. Rāma's wife was king Janaka's daughter Sītā who was endowed both with the beauty of form and generosity of heart. King Janaka had, through the favour of god Śiva, obtained a wonderful bow for the destruction of his enemies. The wise and mighty king proclaimed that whosoever, man, god or demon, succeeded in straining the bow would be given the hand of Sītā. The valiant Rāma, having known this and having gone to the abode of Janaka, lifted the bow without effort and bent it till it snapped in two. The righteous hero then married Sītā as Śiva had married Pārvatī and carried her with him as Skanda carries the divine army with him.

It is noteworthy that this account, though clearly mentioning the visit of Rāma to the palace of Janaka, omits all mention of Viśvāmitra[8] and this is as it should be, for the sage Viśvāmitra was an early Ṛgvedic *ṛṣi* who lived centuries before Rāma in the time of his ancestor Hariścandra. It is probable that on their journey to the capital of king Janaka, Rāma and Lakṣmaṇa were accompanied by a certain sage belonging to the Kauśika *gotra* who was later mistaken for Viśvāmitra.[9] The testimony of the *Kūrma Purāṇa* thus makes it possible to differentiate the genuine cantos of the *Bālakāṇḍa* from the spurious ones which we shall now proceed to do.

The fifth Canto of the *Bālakāṇḍa* certainly forms, as shown convincingly by Jacobi, the commencement of the original poem of Vālmīki, and the following two Cantos form a natural continuation of the matter of this canto. Barring verses 2 and 3 of Canto 11 and verses 45 and 46 of Canto 13, the genuineness of Cantos11, 12 and 13 which describe the performance of a horse sacrifice by king Daśaratha need also not be doubted, for it was natural for the poet to proclaim the glory of the father of his hero as the performer of a horse sacrifice. The next genuine portion of this *kāṇḍa* consists of the first 20 verses of Canto 17 which give an account of the birth and early life of Rāma and his brothers[10] (barring the second hemistichs of verses 6, 8 and 9 which were added after the deification of Rāma and his brothers). Like the first four cantos, the intervening Cantos 8 to 10 giving the legend of Ṛṣyaśṛṅga and Cantos 14 to 16 relating the stories of Viṣṇu's condescension to descend of the earth for the destruction of Rāvaṇa, the performance of *putreṣṭi* sacrifice and the rise of a divine being carrying the miraculous *pāyasa* are undoubtedly interpolated. It is remarkable that the flow of narrative in Cantos 5, 6, 7, 11, 12, 13 and 17 is uninterrupted, and Canto 17 takes no notice of the *putreṣṭi* sacrifice but mentions the horse sacrifice alone. The spuriousness of the Cantos describing the *putreṣṭi* sacrifice is further proved by the fact that there is not the slightest indication anywhere before Canto XIV that Daśaratha intended to perform or was advised to perform this sacrifice.

It is certain that the matter linking the early life of Rāma in Canto 17 and the breaking of the bow by him in canto 66 must have been of the extent of more than a Canto in the original poem of Vālmīki. Some later versifier has, however, spun it out into an account consisting of about 50 Cantos full of absurd myths by mistaking the sage who accompanied Rāma to Mithilā for Viśvāmitra. It is fortunately not impossible to pick out the grain from the husk, and the genuine verses of Vālmīki appear to be embedded in Cantos 21, 22, 30, 44, 49 and 65.[11]

As far as Canto 66 is concerned, the genuine portion of it definitely consists of verses 2 and 3 and 16 to 27 which give a flawless and perfect description of the breaking of the wonderful bow of Janaka by Rāma. Among the ramaining ten cantos of this *kāṇḍa*, the first six are directly connected with the marriage of Rāma. Of these six Cantos 67 to 70 are genuine barring verses

8 and 13 of Canto 67 which were interpolated when the sage accompanying Rāma was identified with Viśvāmitra, and verses 15 and 17 to 31 of Canto 69 which give a garbled pedigree of king Daśaratha.[12] Canto 71 is not only missing in certain manuscripts but is in direct contradiction to Canto 72, for whereas in the former Viśvāmitra is more important than Vasiṣṭha, in the latter Vasiṣṭha alone acts as the priest and Viśvāmitra is not mentioned at all. Canto 71 is therefore spurious barring verses 20 to 24 which must have been originally at the commencemet of Canto 72 that is genuine.

Jacobi's arguments against the genuineness of the cantos describing the marriages of Rāma and his brothers are not quite convincing. It is not possible to believe that Vālmīki, who gives such a detailed description of all the events in the life of Rāma till the time of his coronation, refused to give any account of such an important event as his marriage. Let us therefore dispassionately discuss this matter. This is what Jacobi says to disprove the authenticity of the cantos, describing the marriage of Rāma and his brothers:

> "I shall hold in bold relief only two points. In the first book, we find that Lakṣmaṇa brings to his home his wife Urmilā, the sister of Sītā, but in the second book we do not hear anything about her; yet there must have been the occasion for the mention of Lakṣmaṇa's wife, when Lakṣmaṇa resolved to accompany Rāma and the exiled took leave of their parents. It was the occasion for a very touching scene! But Vālmīki seems to have forgotten the poor Urmīlā because he is not acquainted with her. So he does not make Rāma a liar when the latter at III,18, 3 shows Lakṣmaṇa to Śūrpaṇakhā who wanted to marry him and this he made because Lakṣmaṇa was still then a bachelor (*akṛtadāra*)."

> "The second point concerns about Bharata's absence at

the time when Rāma is banished to the forest. It is supposed in the second book and even expressly mentioned. . . . In the 73rd Canto of the first book it is specially mentioned that Yudhājit comes to see his sister's son Bharata. It happens on the morning of the day of marriage. The four marriages take place but there is no mention of Yudhājit till in the last canto. There Daśaratha allows Bharata and Śatrughna to go with Yudhājit and indeed as the context demands only after the marrige and the return of the party to Ayodhyā. This moment is chosen to be specially suitable for the newly-wedded bridegroom to make a journey to the distant land of Kekaya. But still more striking is the fact that Bharata has passed many years in the distant land, because he is recalled only when Rāma went to the forest."[13]

In plain language what Jacobi wants to say is this. If Rāma and his brothers were married simultaneously and had brought their wives to Ayodhyā immediately after their marriages, as we learn from Cantos 66 to 76 of the first book of the *Rāmāyaṇa*, we are faced with the following questions:

1. Why did Bharata and Śatrughna go to the distant land of Kekaya for 12 long years leaving their newly-married wives behind immediately after their arrival in Ayodhyā with them?
2. Why did Lakṣmaṇa totally forget Urmilā at the time of his departure to the forest with his elder brother Rāma?
3. Why did Rāma describe Lakṣmaṇa as *akṛtadāra* or one not having a wife to Śūrpaṇakhā?

The only answer to these questions according to Jacobi is that these cantos are interpolated and the brothers of Rāma were not yet married at the time of his banishment.

There are, however, certain notable facts which eluded

Jacobi. In the first place it is very important to remember that the hemistich occurring twice in the *Rāmāyaṇa*[14] according to which there was an interval of twelve years between the marriage and banishment of Rāma has another version according to which the interval was of only one year.[15] This second version appears to be more authentic because it is supported by *Rāmāyaṇa,* I,76,14. According to it, Rāma spent many *ṛtu*s or seasons in the company of Sītā in Ayodhyā before his banishment. A *ṛtu* consists of two months and there are six *ṛtu*s in a year. Since Vālmīki is mentioning Rāma's stay in Ayodhyā in the company of Sītā in terms of a small unit of the year[16], it definitely means that the period was actually less than a year. Even if Rāma spent four *ṛtu*s or eight months, one can, when one does not want to be precise, regard this period as roughly equivalent to one year. The reverse, however, is not true, for if Rāma had spent one full year in Ayodhyā in the company of Sītā, Vālmīki would not have called this period as 'many *ṛtu*s'.

The objections raised by Jacobi would, however, still be valid if all the four princes were almost the same age and they all brought their brides to Ayodhyā after their marriages. Let us therefore examine these points also. As far as the age of Rāma at the time of his marriage is concerned, *Rāmāyaṇa*, III,45,10 throws light on it. According to this verse Rāma and Sītā were twenty-five and eighteen year sold respectively at the time of their banishment. Since their banishment took place less than a year after their marriage, they must have been a little over twenty-four and seventeen years of age respectively at the time of their marriage.

We now come to the question of the ages of Rāma's three brothers at the time of their marriages. As has already been shown there is nothing to validate the belief that his brothers were born about the same time as Rāma. We should therefore see if there is any other evidence regarding the ages of the three princes. Luckily some statements occurring in the second book of the *Rāmāyaṇa* throw light on the age of Bharata. In *Rāmāyaṇa,*

II, 8, 19 Mantharā says that Bharata was sent to his maternal uncle's house when he was but a child. In II, 40, 8 Rāma says the same thing about Bharata. If Bharata was not yet an adult at the time of his marriage, it goes without saying that Lakṣmaṇa too, who was younger than Bharata, was not an adult at the time of his marriage. It is quite possible that according to a tradition prevalent among the *sūtas*, Lakṣmaṇa was 15 years of age at the time of his marriage and the interpolator of Canto 19 of the first book regarding Rāma and Lakṣmaṇa to be practically of the same age, attributed the age of Laksmaṇa to Rāma, unmindful of the age of Rāma mentioned in the *Araṇyakāṇḍa*. The admonition of Sumitrā to Lakṣmaṇa at the time of his departure to forest to treat Rāma and Sītā like his father and mother also shows that Laksmaṇa at that time was of a tender age and younger than both Rāma and Sītā. Thus it appears that while Rāma and Sītā were adults at the time of their marriage, this was not the case with Rāma's brothers and their brides.

For millenniums it has been the custom in India that when a couple is not yet adult at the time of marriage, the bride is not sent to her husband's home until she attains adolescence. In order to make the bonds of the royal families of Ayodhyā and Mithilā as strong as possible, the three younger brothers of Rāma were also married in the royal family of Mithilā at the same time as their elder brother even though they were not yet of marriageable age. The brides of the three princes, therefore, must have stayed back in their paternal home after their marriage. Verses 8 to 11 of the last Canto of the first book which mention the arrival of all the brides in Ayodhyā are definitely interpolated, for there is never again a mention of any of these princesses in the following book of the *Rāmāyaṇa* even when there is occasion for it.

We thus see that Bharata and Śatrughna did not have to leave their brides behind in Ayodhyā at the time of their departure to the kingdom of Kekaya. Similarly the silence of

Vālmīki about Urmilā at the time of Lakṣmaṇa's departure to forest is not because Lakṣmaṇa was not yet married but because Urmilā was not in Ayodhyā even after her marriage.

We have yet to answer the question of Jacobi whether Vālmīki makes Rāma a liar when the latter in III, 17, 3 shows Lakṣmaṇa to Śūrpaṇakhā and describes him as *akṛtadāra*, i.e. one not having a wife. There are two things which conclusively prove that this equivocal statement was made jocularly and not with the intention of concealing the truth. The first thing which should be taken note of is that according to III, 17, 1 Rāma made this statement smilingly.[17] The second thing which leaves no room for doubt about Rāma's intention is that later in III, 17, 19 he makes a regretful observation that it is a mistake to crack jokes with savage barbarians.[18]

Finally we must take up Cantos 73, 74, 75 and 76 of the *Bālakāṇḍa* for discussion. Cantos 73 to 75 of this *kāṇḍa* are definitely spurious. These cantos contain the episode of Paraśurāma's discomfiture by Rāma. That this episode is anachronistic does not admit of any doubt, for Paraśurāma lived much earlier than Rāma as is proved by the mention of his father Jamadagni as a contemporary of Rāma's distant ancestor Hariścandra in the *Aitereya Brāhmaṇa*. The question, however, is whether this episode occurred in the original *Rāmāyaṇa* of Vālmīki. The late origin of this episode is proved by the fact that none of the earliest Purāṇas giving the story of the *Rāmāyaṇa* such as the *Kūrma*, the *Garuḍa*, the *Brahma* and the *Hārivaṁśa* know it. The three cantos of the *Rāmāyaṇa* which contain this episode are therefore undoubtedly interpolated. Canto 76 is genuine barring verses 8 to 11 mentioning the arrival of all four brides in Ayodhyā.

The genuine portion of the *Bālakāṇḍa* was thus not of the length of more than 15 Cantos, and must have formed a part of the *Ayodhyākāṇḍa*, which as rightly observed by Jacobi, must have originally been the first book of the *Rāmāyaṇa*.

The Purāṇas clearly indicate, the stages in the growth of *Bālakāṇḍa*. The first two cantos of this *kāṇḍa*, containing the table of contents of the original poem, and the episode of the origin of the *śloka* meter, must have been the earliest ones to be interpolated. Cantos 14 to 16, which declare Rāma to be an incarnation of Viṣṇu, must have closely followed the first two Cantos since, barring the *Vāyu* and the *Brahmāṇḍa*, all the Purāṇas which give the story of Rāma regard him as an incarnation of Viṣṇu. Rāma's association with Viśvāmitra, which is unknown to the *Kūrma Purāṇa* is mentioned for the first time by the *Brahma* and *Garuḍa Purāṇa*s and the *Harivaṁśa*. Most of the matter of the *Bālakāṇḍa* from the latter part of Canto 17 to Canto 65 describing the journey of Rāma and Lakṣmaṇa under the guidance of Viśvāmitra, must therefore have been, the next portion to be included in this *kāṇḍa*. The story of Paraśurāma's discomfiture by Rāma, which is unknown to the *Kūrma*, the *Brahma*, and the *Garuḍa Purāṇa*s and the *Harivaṁśā,* is first mentioned by *Viṣṇu Purāṇa*. The last interpolation of the *Bālakāṇḍa* thus indisputably consisted of Cantos 73 to 75 which give the episode of Paraśurāma, besides Cantos 8 to 10, which gives the legend of Ṛṣyaśṛṅga and Cantos 3 and 4, which give a new table of contents, and relate the myth of singing of the *Rāmāyaṇa* by Kuśa and Lava.

As stated earlier, some Cantos, episodes, and verses have been interpolated even in the genuine five books of the *Rāmāyaṇa*. Once such episode occurs in the *Sundarakāṇḍa*, which has been given this name because in it Hanumat brings the good news about the whereabouts and safety of Sītā to Rāma. This episode is the destruction of the Aśokagrove, and the subsequent burning of Laṅkā by Hanumat. These acts are certainly not in consonance with the character of Hanumat, whose utterances and actions are always marked by wisdom, dignity and sobriety.

It seems that some interpolators, misled by the term *Vānara* and its synonyms applied to Hanumat in the *Rāmāyaṇa*, fancifully attributed to him the wantom destruction of the Aśokagrove and the subsequent incredible feat of burning of every house in Laṅkā while remaining unsathed himself, and yet not provoking Rāvaṇa to take revenge against him or Sītā. That this later fabrication has been proved beyond a shadow of doubt by Professor Jacobi, whose arguments are given below:

1. In the long conversation between him and Sītā in Canto 38, Hanumat does not give the slightest hint about his intention of plunging into the adventure ascribed to him in the following Cantos, but takes leave of her with the assurance that he would convey her message to Rāma, and even takes her crest-jewel to be given to her husband as proof of his finding out and meeting Sītā. The question that naturally occurs to any intelligent reader is this: where was this jewel when Hanumat was having a scuffle with the *rākṣasas* in the Aśokagrove when he was taken captive before Rāvaṇa and when he was setting fire to the houses of Laṅkā? The inevitable conclusion is that this whole episode, as described in the following sixteen Cantos, is the figment of the imagination of some interpolator who, having made Hanumat to stay in Laṅkā even after he had taken leave of Sītā, was forced to make him take leave of her again in Canto 54.

2. After his return to Rāma, Hanumat reports to him all that has happened between him and Sītā (V, 63-66), but he does not mention here anything about the destruction of the Aśoka grove and burning of Laṅkā by him. He also mentions Sītā's request to him to stay incognito for one day more. This request is quite natural to one whose identity is unknown to Rāvaṇa, but becomes ridiculous to one who has gravely offended Rāvaṇa by burning his city.

3. When Rāma besieged Laṅkā, it stood in its total splendour although not more than a month had elapsed since the

burning of the city by Hanumat, which is thus proved to be totally fake.

4. A further evidence against the genuineness of the episode of the Hanumat's scuffle with *rākṣasas* and burning of Laṅkā is that in Canto 44, which embodies a portion of the entire story, we find the description of the killing of the two heroes Yūpākṣa and Virūpākṣa by Hanumat, but the same heroes are found to have remained alive later and their death is described in Cantos 76 and 96 of the sixth book.

5. Finally, in his report to Bharata about Rāma's experiences, Hanumat mentions only giving of Rāma's ring to Sītā and bringing to Rāma the crest-jewel[19] of Sītā, but makes no reference to his adventures in Laṅkā.

The spuriousness of the episode of the burning of Laṅkā by Hanumat is not only proved by the internal evidence of the *Rāmāyaṇa* but also by the external evidence of the Purāṇas a little earlier.

The stroy of Rāma is found in nine Purāṇas. Of these, the older six Purāṇas, namely the *Vāyu*, the *Brahmāṇḍa*, the *Kūrma*, the *Brahma*, the *Garuḍa* and the *Viṣṇu* do not at all mention the episode of burning of Laṅkā by Hanumat. The *Harivaṁśa* is also silent about this episode in its story of Rāma. Only the three latest Purāṇas, the *Bhāgavata*, the *Agni*, and the *Padma* mention this episode, which is also referred to in the comparatively late *Rāmopākhyāna* of the *Mahābhārata*. The non-mention of this episode in six of the oldest Purāṇas and the *Harivaṁśa* clearly proves that it was interpolated in the *Rāmāyaṇa* after the composition of these works.

The proof given by Jacobi for the spuriousness of the present last book of the *Rāmāyaṇa* has already been mentioned above. Additional arguments in support of it can be seen in the second chapter of this book.

The characters, choosen to show how in the course of centuries their real story was completely transformed, are all very well known and held in the highest esteem by Hindus. Yet they are so much enveloped in myths, invented at a very late period, that their very historicity has become a subject of doubt. The object of this book is to show that these myths are at complete variance with the ancient evidence regarding these great men of the most ancient period of Indian history.

References

1. See chapter VII of my book *India in the Vedic Age*, 2nd edn. (Lucknow, 1971).
2. McCrindle, *Ancient India: The Indika of Arrian*, Chapter IX, para 2.
3. *India in the Vedic Age*, 2nd edn., pp. 57-58.
4. See *Das Rāmāyaṇa*, English translation by S.N. Ghosal, published by Oriental Institute, Baroda, 1960, pp. 42-43.
5. It should be remembered that the non-mention even of the genuine matter of the *Bālakāṇḍa* consisting of the description of Ayodhyā and the birth and marriage of Rāma in the table of contents given in Canto I of that *kāṇḍa* is due to the fact that the author of this Canto is actually recounting those events of Rāma's life which made him an ideal hero and not merely giving a list of the contents of the epic.
6. *Kūrma*, I. 21. 17-53; *Brahma,* 213. 124-158; *Garuḍa,* I. 142. 10-18; *Viṣṇu,* IV,4,86-104; *Agni,* 5-11; *Bhāgavata,* IX,10 and 11; *Padma*, VI,42-44; *Harivaṁśa,* I,41, 21-55; *Mahābhārata* III,273-91.
7. The mention of the worship of Śivaliṅga by Rāma on the bridge built for crossing over to Laṅkā is proof only of the strong Śaivite character of this Purāṇa and does not by any means stand in the way of its being one of the older Purāṇas.
8. One can understand the omission of Lakṣmaṇa in the brief account of Rāma's visit to the court of Janaka given by this Purāṇa, but if Rāma had proceeded under the guidance of Viśvāmitra, the Purāṇa could not have shown its irreverence to an eminent sage like him by totally ignoring him. The late Canto 3 of

book I of the *Rāmāyaṇa* in its list of contents takes care to mention the name of Viśvāmitra in connection with Rāma's journey to Mithilā, though ignoring the name of Lakṣmaṇa.

9. Since the descendants of the ancient *ṛṣi* Vasiṣṭha bore the *gotra* name Vasiṣṭha it is possible that the priest of king Daśaratha was called Vasiṣṭha after his *gotra*. Viśvāmitra was, however, never the name of a *gotra* and so the question of the sage who accompanied Rāma and Lakṣmaṇa to the capital of Janaka being Viśvāmitra does not arise.

10. In the seventeenth Canto of the *Bālakāṇḍa* the critical edition of the *Rāmāyaṇa* has created a lacuna by omitting the verses which form a natural link between the departure of Ṛṣyaśṛṅga (in verse 5) and the birth of Rāma. In view of this as well as of the well established tradition regarding the birth of Rāma on the 9th of the bright fortnight of *Caitra*, it is certain that at least the first two verses given against 506* on p.122 of the critical edition must have formed part of the authentic text of Vālmīki.

11. See Appendix at the end of the book.

12. Since in Canto 70 Janaka has been clearly made to say that one who gives his daughter in marriage must speak out the particulars of his family to the bridegroom's elders, it is clear that Vālmīki mentioned only the pedigree of Janaka and the pedigree of Daśaratha in the preceding Canto was added much later by some ingnorant interpolater.

13. *Das Rāmāyaṇa* of H. Jacobi, translated from German by S.N. Ghosal.

14. III,45,4 and V,31,13. The hemistich which has been put in the mouth of Sītā is as follows with slight variations:

    समा द्वादश तत्रासं राघवस्य निवेशने।

15. This version is as follows with slight variations:

    संवत्सरं चाध्युषिता राघवस्य निवेशने ।

    It is strange that the critical edition of the *Rāmāyaṇa* published by Oriental Institute Baroda, which has been used in this book for references, accepts this version in III,45,4, but accepts the other version in V,31,13.

16. It is bigger only than a month. If Vālmīki had stated the period

in terms of months, nobody would have thought of this period as equal to even one year.

17. तां तु शूर्पणखां रामः कामपाश विपाशिताम् ।
स्वेच्छया श्लक्ष्णया वाचा स्मितपूर्वमथाब्रवीत् ।।

18. क्रूरैरनार्यैः सौमित्रे परिहासः कथंचन ।
न कार्यः पश्च वैदेहीं कथंचित् सौम्य जीवतीम् ।।

— Rāmāyaṇa, VI, 126.

2

Did Rāma Banish his Wife Sītā?

Rāma, the hero of the epic composed by Vālmīki has been regarded by the Hindus for millenniums as the embodiment of virtue and the model to be followed in all spheres of man's life. The earliest mention of a mighty king bearing the name Rāma is found in a hymn of the tenth book of the *Ṛgveda* and this is in conformity with the genealogical account of the Purāṇas which makes it clear that this great hero lived in the Vedic age. It is, however, to be deplored that, notwithstanding the fact that Rāma lived in the Vedic age, no work belonging to that period gives even the briefest reference to any incident of his life. The earliest works which give some account of this mighty hero are nine of the eighteen Purāṇas, the *Rāmāyaṇa* of Vālmīki, the *Mahābhārata*, the *Harivaṁśa* and the Buddhist *Dasaratha Jātaka*. As proved by Jacobi, the last mentioned work contains only a garbled version of the *Rāmāyaṇa* and thus the only works to be depended on are the Purāṇas, the *Harivaṁśa*, the *Rāmāyaṇa* and the *Mahābhārata*.

Though the genealogical account of the present Purāṇas is based on that of the original *Purāṇa Saṁhitā* embodying the matter handed down by the *sūtas*, it should not be forgotten that since these works were composed at widely different times the account found in them has, with numerous additions and interpolations made from time to time, grown into something vastly different from that found in the original work. The oldest of the present Purāṇas are the *Vāyu* and its counterpart *Brahmāṇḍa*. The account of Rāma as found in them[1] is as follows:

King Daśaratha, a scion of the family of Ikṣvākus and ruler of Ayodhyā, had four sons named Rāma, Bharata, Lakṣmaṇa and Śatrughna. Of these, Rāma the eldest was noted for his handsome appearance and noble qualities. His wife was Sītā who,while he was living in Janasthāna, was abducted by Rāvaṇa. Tracing out the way by which Sītā was carried, Rāma attacked and killed Rāvaṇa. He then ruled over Ayodhyā for a long time.[2] He was an ideal king in whose dominion there was constant chanting of the Vedas made possible by the protection given to the subjects by the twang of his bow. There was also great material prosperity and everyone both enjoyed and gave away things in plenty. Rāma had two sons named Kuśa and Lava. The former succeeded him to the throne of Ayodhyā, while his other son and the sons of his brothers carved out new kingdoms for themselves.

There can be hardly any doubt that this account of Rāma found in the *Vāyu* and *Brahmāṇḍa Purāṇas* is a concise version of the story of Rāma occurring in the original *Purāṇa Saṁhitā*. The other Purāṇas as well as the *Harivaṁśa* and the *Mahābhārata* have followed the *Rāmāyaṇa* of Vālmīki for their versions of the story of Rāma. Thus the oldest of the remaining Purāṇas, viz., the *Matsya* clearly calls the biographer of Rāma as Vālmīki, whose name also occurs in some other Purāṇas and the *Mahābhārata*.[3] As we are concerned only with the story of the banishment of Sītā by Rāma, we now propose to discuss it threadbare.

This story which has most surprisingly penetrated into every village and hamlet of India, is found in the seventh book of the *Rāmāyaṇa*, called the *Uttarakāṇḍa*. This book contains a number of myths concerning Rāvaṇa and other prominent figures of ancient times, many of whom are well-known in the

Purāṇas. But the central theme of the book is the exile of Sītā and the slaying of the Śūdra ascetic Śambūka by Rāma. The spurious nature of the entire *Uttarakāṇḍa* is indubitably established by the unimpeachable evidence of the last canto of the *Yuddhakāṇḍa*.

After a charming account of the coronation of Rāma and Sītā, this Canto not only gives a glowing description of the peace, prosperity, and piety that prevailed in the kingdom of Kosala during the reign of Rāma, but also mentions the promise of the reward [*śravaṇaphala*] which is assigned to those who would hear the *Rāmāyaṇa*. This is the clearest proof of the fact that the poem of Vālmīki ended here, because the śravaṇaphala is always given at the end of a poem.

So far as the central theme of the *Uttarakāṇḍa* is concerned we are fortunate in possessing the additional testimony of the *Mahābhārata* and the Purāṇas. A study of these works conclusively establishes that the central theme of the *Uttarakāṇḍa* is not only unauthentic but also a very late invention. The *Rāmopākhyāna* of the *Mahābhārata* gives a fairly detailed story of Rāma but is silent about the banishment of Sītā and the slaying of the śūdra ascetic by Rāma.[4] The *Harivaṁśa* and the *Vāyu*, *Brahmāṇḍa*, *Kūrma*, *Garuḍa* and *Viṣṇu Puraṇā*s also give the story of Rāma but are totally unaware of the banishment of Sītā and the slaying of the śūdra ascetic by him. These myths had not yet come into existence even when Bhāsa wrote his Rāma plays. The earliest works which mention the incident of the banishment of Sītā by Rāma are the *Gautamīmāhātmya* of the *Brahma Purāṇa*[5], the *Agni*, *Bhāgavata* and *Padma Purāṇa*s and the *Raghuvaṁśa* of Kālidāsa. The slaying of śūdra ascetic Śambūka is mentioned only in the last two works.[6] The inevitable conclusion is that the incident of Sītā's exile by Rāma was invented at a very late period, while the tale of Śambūka arose later still. The date of the rise of these myths could not have been earlier than the fourth century A.D.

The central theme of the *Uttarakāṇḍa*, is discredited not only by the internal evidence of the *Rāmāyaṇa* and the external evidence of the *Mahābhārata*, the *Harivaṁśa* and the ancient Purāṇas, but is also inconsistent with some other facts. Having commended the *tapas* of a woman of the lowly *śabara* tribe in III,70,7, Rāma could not have punished a man of the śūdra caste, for the same act of piety.

So far as the banishment of Sītā is concerned, it does not take note of the fact that from the report given by Hanumat, the people of Ayodhyā must have been convinced about the purity of Sītā, and so there was no question of any murmur arising among them.

In summing up we can say that besides the testimony of Hanumat, two very important facts lead us to the inevitable conclusion that the stories of Sītā's banishment and the slaying of the śūdra ascetic Śambūka by Rāma were invented at a very late period.

These two facts are as follows:

(1) The *Rāmāyaṇa* has been concluded at the end of its sixth book named *Yuddhakāṇḍa* pointing to the fact that its last book named *Uttarakāṇḍa*, containing the stories of Sītā's banishment and the slaying of Śambūka, was a later addition.

(2) The *Mahābhārata*, the *Harivaṁśa*, and five of the ancient *Purāṇas*, viz., *Vāyu, Brahmāṇḍa, Kūrma, Garuḍa* and *Vīsṇu* which give the story of Rāma are silent about the incidents of the banishment of Sītā and the slaying of the śūdra ascetic by him.

The evidence against the genuineness of the story of Sītā's banishment by Rāma is so overwhelming that one really feels flabbergasted on seeing not only layman but even scholars harping on it.

It is, to say the least, the gravest of injustic to Rāma that is being perpetrated by the very people who claim to adore him.

References

1. *Vāyu*, 88, 184 to 200; *Brahmāṇḍa*, III, 63, 185 to 200. Although like the other Purāṇas the *Vāyu* and the *Brahmāṇḍa* also in their present form belong to a period when Rāma had already been deified, yet the account of Rāma occurring in the Ikṣvāku genealogy of these Purāṇas appears to be quite ancient.
2. Rāma is said to have ruled for eleven thousand or sixteen thousand years according to the different readings of a verse occurring in the *Rāmāyaṇa*, the Purāṇas and the *Dasaratha Jātaka*. Whereas the other events of Rāma's life, for example, his long exile for 14 years, are mentioned in figures compatible with the human span of life, it is difficult to understand why an exceedingly exaggerated figure has been given for his reign period alone. Did the original tradition transmit the measurement of Rāma's reign period in days (*vāras*) rather than years (*varṣas*)? If so, Rāma must have ruled for eleven thousand days (30 years) as counted from his coronation and sixteen thousand days (44 years) as counted from the death of Daśaratha.
3. *Matsya* 12, 51; *Viṣṇu* III, 3, 18; *Padma* V, 8, 115; *Agni* 273, 35; *Mahābhārata* XII, 57, 40.
4. The fact that the legend of Rāvaṇa as given in the *Rāmopākhyāna* of the *Mahābhārata* agrees in certain respects and differs in others with the one occurring in the *Uttarakāṇḍa* of the *Rāmāyaṇa* only shows that the authors of both have used the same sources and picked up what suited their fancies. It by no means proves the acquaintance of the authors of the *Rāmopākhyāna* with the *Uttarakāṇḍa* of the *Rāmāyaṇa*.
5. It is remarkable that the original *Brahma Purāṇa* in its story of the *Rāmāyaṇa* makes no mention of the banishment of Sītā, and only the *Gautamīmāhātmya* (chapters70-175) which was at a very late date incorporated in the *Brahma Purāṇa*, refers to it in chapter 154.
6. It is also passingly referred to in verse 67 of a late tale entitled "A dialogue between the Vulture and the Jackal", occurring in *Mahābhārata,* XII,153.

3

Did Rāma kill Bālin Surreptitiously?

THE episode of the death of Bālin, at the hands of Rāma occurs in Cantos XII to XXV of the fourth book of the *Rāmāyaṇa*, known as the *Kiṣkindhākāṇḍa*.

In the absence of a critical and comparative study of the *Rāmāyaṇa* and the Purāṇas, it has been held for hundreds of years, on the basis of the cantos XVI, XVII, XVIII of the *Kiṣkindhākāṇḍa*, that Rāma killed Bālin surreptitiously. But according to other parts of the *Rāmāyaṇa* itself, which have unfortunately received scant attention so far, Bālin was killed in a battle between him and Rāma.

The relevant passages are as follows:

The first canto of the first book of the *Rāmāyaṇa*, while giving the contents of the epic, clearly says that Rāma killed Bālin in a battle.[1] In the fifth book again Hanumat tells Sītā that Rāma killed Bālin in a battle.[2] Hanumat again says the same thing to Bharata at the end of the sixth book.[3]

These statements of the *Rāmāyaṇa* find support in the story of Rāma, occurring in the *Harivaṁśa* and the *Brahma Purāṇa*s. An identical verse[4] found in these two works says that Rāma, having killed Bālin in a battle, crowned Sugrīva as king in his place.

What is most intriguing in this connection is the fact that canto XIX of the *Kiśkindhākāṇḍa,* going against the version of the earlier cantos, gives an account of the battle between Rāma and Bālin in verses 11 to 13. When Tārā, the wife of Bālin, expresses her suspicion that Rāma killed Bālin from a far off place with his far reaching arrows, the *vānara*s give the following reply:

> (Thank God that) your son is living. Go back and protect him. Yama, assuming the shape of Rāma, has killed Bālin. Having pierced trees and big rocks hurled at him, Rāma killed Bālin with his sharp arrows resembling the thunderbolt. When that lion among Vānaras having the glow of Indra, was killed, the defeated army of Vānaras fled away.[5]

Here a battle between Rāma and Bālin has been described in unequivocal language. The question naturally arises as to why there is no reference to any such battle in canto 16. The only possible answer is that some verses describing the battle between Rāma and Bālin which preceded the present verse 25 of canto 16 of the *Kiṣkindhākāṇḍa* were very early lost. With the loss of these verses a misunderstanding naturally arose that Rāma killed Bālin without any warning. This gave rise to several explanatory interpolations, resulting in a number of contradictions in the story of Bālin and his brother Sugrīva occurring in cantos XII to XIX of the *Kiṣkindhākāṇḍa*, which we shall now discuss.

A critical study of these cantos makes it absolutely clear that most of the matter of cantos XII, XIV, XVII and XVIII is interpolated. In canto XII all the matter following verse 13 is clearly interpolated, because according to it, Rāma has already arrived in Kiṣkindhā, whereas in the following canto, he is still shown to be on the Ṛṣyamūka hill, from where his journey to Kiṣkindhā is described. The fourteenth canto is likewise interpolated, barring verses 2 and 3 which are clearly related to canto XV and were originally at its beginning.[6]

The seventeenth and eighteenth cantos are indubitably interpolated. When once the misgiving that Bālin was killed by Rāma without any warning had been firmly established, it was natural for interpolators to feel that this episode would be incomplete without showing Bālin's condemnation of Rāma's action and Rāma's reply to it. These cantos were added to fill this supposed lacuna, and to establish a superficial connection of these cantos with the genuine canto XIX, a verse was interpolated at the beginning of the latter.

The inconsistencies that arose as a result of these interpolations are too glaring to be missed by any intelligent reader. Many proofs can be adduced to show the interpolated nature of cantos XVII and XVIII. Thus in the sixteenth canto Bālin is said to have fallen unconscious as a result of the arrow shot at him by Rāma. There is, however, not the least sign of this unconsciousness in the seventeenth canto. On the contrary as soon as Rāma approaches Bālin after shooting the arrow at him, the latter begins to talk with Rāma. The second proof of the interpolated nature of these two cantos is that canto XIX follows the events of canto XVI and not those of these two cantos. Thus in canto XVIII Rāma is pacified after his dialogue with Bālin and so the fleeing of the *Vānaras* through fear of Rāma as described in canto XIX has no *raison d'être*. On the other hand, the event of Bālin falling unconscious after being pierced by the arrow of Rāma as described in canto XVI is again referred to in canto XIX, thus showing its direct connection with canto XVI. When we realize this connection between canto XVI and canto XIX, the fleeing of *Vānaras* through fear of Rāma as described in the latter canto is full understandable. The third proof of the interpolated nature of cantos XVII and XVIII is that according to the first verse of canto XXII, Bālin, after being struck by the arrow of Rāma, first saw Sugrīva and not Rāma or Lakṣmaṇa as appears from canto XVII. Since the description of events following the shooting of Bālin as found in canto XIX of *Kiṣkindhākāṇḍa* is in disagreement only with the interpolated portions mentioned above, the removal of these portions frees the episode of Bālin of all contradictions and establishes the fact that, according to the genuine account of the *Rāmāyaṇa*, Rāma killed Bālin in a battle provoked by the latter's attack on him.

References

1. ततः सुग्रीववचनाद्धत्वा बालिनमाहवे ।
   सुग्रीवमेव राज्ये राघवः प्रत्यपादयत् ।। — *Rāmāyaṇa*, I,1,55
2. ततो निहत्य तरसा रामो बालिन माहवे ।
   सर्वर्क्षहरिसंघानां सुग्रीवमकरोत्पतिम् ।। — *Rāmāyaṇa,* V,35,50
3. रामः स्वबाहुवीर्येण स्वराज्यं प्रत्यपादयत् ।
   बालिनं समरे हत्वा महाकायं महाबलम्।। — *Rāmāyaṇa,* VI,126, 38
4. सुग्रीवस्य कृते येन वानरेन्द्रो महाबलः ।
   बाली विनिहितो युद्धे सुग्रीवश्चाभिषेचिता ।।
   — *Harivaṁśa* I,41, 133, *Brahma* 213,136
5. जीवपुत्रे निवर्तस्व, पुत्रं रक्षस्व चाङ्गदम् ।
   अन्तको रामरूपेण, हत्वा नयति बालिनम् ।।

   क्षिप्तान् वृक्षान् समाविध्य विपुलाश्च तथा शिलाः ।
   बाली वज्रसमैर्वाणैर्वज्रेनेव निपातितः ।।
6. To establish some sort of connection between the interpolated canto XIV and the follcwing genuine canto, verses 9 and 10 were interpolated in the latter.

4

Was Viśvāmitra the Father of Śakuntalā?

VIŚVĀMITRA was one of the greatest *ṛṣis* or Āryan prophets of the Vedic age. He was a poet, a sage and a person of great spiritual attainment who did not hesitate to choose the ecclesiastical order in preference to the heirship of a kingdom. His great qualities of head and heart are amply known from the hymns of the third book of the *Ṛgveda* which owes its existence to him and the various members of his family. Some of the more poetic pieces of the *Ṛgveda* notably the lively dialogue between the poet and the rivers in hymn III,33 and the charming invocation of Dawn in III,61, were composed by Viśvāmitra. Above all he was the author of the most famous Hindu prayer known as Gāyatrī after the metre in which it was composed. He was held in great respect by his contemporaries. According to the *Ṛgveda* he was for sometime the high priest of king Sudās in whose welfare he showed active concern.[1] The *Aitareya Brāhmaṇa* informs us that when king Hariścandra performed a *rājasūya* sacrifice the offices of the four priests viz., Hotṛ, Udgātṛ, Adhvaryu and Brahmā were held by Viśvāmitra, Ayāsya, Jamadagni and Vasiṣṭha respectively. The humane outlook of Viśvāmitra as well as the largeness of his heart is revealed by an incident of this sacrifice which deserves to be mentioned.

In order to please God Varuṇa, through whose favour he had obtained a son, king Hariścandra got bound to the stake a certain boy named Śunaḥśepa whom his heartless father had given away to the king in return for a hundred cows. While the great *ṛṣis* present on the occasion refused to be a party to the inhuman deed, Śunaḥśepa pleased the god by his prayers and was freed from the stake. Since the boy was not willing to go back to his cruel and greedy father, Viśvāmitra, although he had already a number of sons, gladly adopted him and gave him the new name of Devarāta. He carried the adoption to its logical conclusion by bidding his sons to share their inheritance with him.[2]

Another incident showing the magnanimity of Viśvāmitra is mentioned by the Purāṇas in their account of the Ikṣvāku genealogy. Hariścandra's father Triśaṅku was a profligate prince who was banished by his father from the kingdom for abducting another man's wife. His life in the wilderness caused a change of heart and he showed great courtesy to the sage Viśvāmitra who happened to come in contact with him. Finding that the prince was repentant, the generous sage used his good offices to restore him to the throne.This restoration was interpreted by later mythmakers to mean that Viśvāmitra transported him bodily to heaven. The fact that Viśvāmitra and Vasiṣṭha cooperated in the sacrifice performed by Triśaṅku's son proves the baselessness of the allegation of some of the Purāṇas that Viśvāmitra restored Triśaṅku to the throne in the teeth of the opposition of Vasiṣṭha.

Viśvāmitra was a descendant of the celebrated king Jahnu who, being the first Āryan ruler to found a kingdom on the bank of the river Gaṅgā, proudly gave his name to the river which came to be called Jāhnavī.[3] One of the descendants of Jahnu was the famous Kuśika whose son king Gāthin or Gādhi was the father of Viśvāmitra. The capital of the kingdom of Gāthin was Kānyakubja, the modern Kannauj, which must have been the birthplace of Viśvāmitra. As already pointed out, Viśvāmitra renounced the kingdom in consequence of his spiritual bent of mind. Thus from a kṣatriya he became a brāhmaṇa and founded the Kauśika family of brāhmaṇs named after his grandfather Kuśika.

It is a pity that the Purāṇas and the *Mahābhārata* have given divergent accounts of Jahnu's ancestors. Jahnu was well-known as Sauhotri, i.e., son or descendant of Suhotra. This Suhotra has, however, been identified with two different persons in two different accounts and consequently we have two versions of the lineage of Viśvāmitra. According to the *Mahābhārata* as also the *Harivaṁśa* and the *Brahma* and *Agni Purāṇas*, Viśvāmitra was born on the lineage of Suhotra, a near descendant of king Bharata, son of Duṣyanta. But according to another version found in the *Vāyu*, *Brahmāṇḍa*, *Viṣṇu*, *Garuḍa* and *Bhāgavata Purāṇas* he was born in the lineage of Suhotra, a near descendant of king Purūravas, who lived long before Bharata. Luckily the Vedic literature comes to our rescue and makes it clear that the former version is correct. In the *Ṛgveda* Viśvāmitra himself speaks of his family's descent from Bharata.[4] In the *Aitareya Brāhmaṇa* he is called Bharata *ṛṣabha*, i.e., best among the Bharatas.[5] The *Śāṅkhāyana Śrauta Sūtra* similarly calls him Bharata *ṛṣabha*.[6] There is thus no room for doubt that Viśvāmitra was a descendant of the famous king Bharata, son of Duṣyanta.

The funniest thing which late myth makers have done is that while inventing myths they have sometimes been totally oblivious of the inconsistency of these myths with the original matter of the work in which they were interpolating them. The *Mahābhārata* in two different books far separated from each other makes it absolutely clear that Jahnu and his descendants Kuśikas, among whom the most noted was Viśvāmitra, were born in the lineage of Bharata, son of Duṣyanta.[7] Yet a late interpolator who wrote up chapters 68-74 of the first book of the *Mahābhārata* containing the story of Duṣyanta has introduced a tale about Viśvāmitra in which the great *ṛṣi* is said to have been the father of Śakuntalā, the mother of Bharata. Thus the king, who according to the genealogy of Viśvāmitra occurring twice in the *Mahābhārata* was an ancestor of the great sage, has been turned into his grandson in a story occurring in the same epic. The story which has been put in the mouth of Śakuntalā is as follows:

> Viśvāmitra once performed such formidable *tapas* or austerities that Indra, the king of gods, was frightened lest he should be deprived of his throne by the sage. He, therefore, sent down a nymph named Menakā to disturb the sage's austerities. When Viśvāmitra saw her peerless beauty he fell in love with her and, forgetting his austerities, succumbed to the pleasures of her company. As a result of this Menakā gave birth to Śakuntalā. With her purpose accomplished Menakā then departed to heaven leaving Śakuntalā on the bank of the river Mālinī, from where the *ṛṣi* Kaṇva picked her up.

This story is not found in any of the Purāṇas except the late *Bhāgavata*.[8] The only reason why this obscure story gained access to the ordinary student of Sanskrit is the fact that the great poet Kālidāsa chanced to refer to it in his world-famous play *Abhijñāna-Śākuntalam*. Apart from the fact that it is inconsistent with the pedigree of Viśvāmitra found not only in the *Mahābhārata* and a number of Purāṇas but also in the Vedic literature, it also violates the ideas of the time when Viśvāmitra lived. Viśvāmitra was a Ṛgvedic *ṛṣi* and the idea of *tapas* by self-mortification did not exist in that period. Even the *Bhagavad gītā* which forms one of the older parts of the *Mahābhārata* discountenances *tapas* by self-mortification.[9] Secondly the conception of Indra as found in this story is diametrically opposed to that found in the *Ṛgveda*. In the *Ṛgveda* Indra is the mightiest of gods to whom the *ṛṣi* Viśvāmitra himself has addressed more than a score of hymns. To depict the *ṛṣi*, who considered praying to Indra as his greatest religious duty, as one who inspired fear in the god by his austerities is nothing but a travesty of truth.

It is thus clear form both the untenability of this story as well as the true genealogy of Viśvāmitra that he was not the father of Śakuntalā but her distant descendant through her son Bharata. The anecdote of his dalliances with Menakā is a mendacious myth that has undeservedly clouded his spiritual greatness.

Two other stories about this great sage, which were invented by half-educated priests and interpolated in the epics and Purāṇas, are the one concerning the long conflict betwen him and the sage Vasiṣṭha,[10] and the one mentioning the terrible ordeal of king Hariścandra at his hands. None of these stories find any support from the Vedic literature, even though this literature refers to Viśvāmitra's close association with both Vasiṣṭha and Hariścandra. So far as the first myth is concerned, it appears that at some post-Vedic period a rivalry developed between the Kauśika and the Vasiṣṭha families and it was projected backwards into a rivalry between Viśvāmitra and Vasiṣṭha, so much so that the last four verses of hymn III,53 ascribed to Viśvāmitra were understood as referring to this rivalry, although there is not the slightest indication of this in the verses. The second myth is, of course, wholly baseless.[11] Lastly it should be remembered that Viśvāmitra being a contemporary of Hariścandra, could not at the same time be a contemporary of the latter's distant descendant Rāma, as the *Rāmāyaṇa* would have us believe.[12]

References

1. *R̥gveda* III, 53. There is no warrant for the assumption of the authors of *Vedic Index* (Vol. II, p. 275) that Viśvāmitra was deposed by Sudās from the post of *purohita* and joined Sudās' enemies. Viśvāmitra perhaps had to quit the office because of illness or death and then Sudās appointed Vasiṣṭha to fill it.
2. *Aitareya Brāhmaṇa* 33.
3. The Purāṇas have unfortunately mythologized this glorious event, but luckily *Mahābhārata* XIII, 4, containing an ancient account of the family of Viśvāmitra, makes the simple statement that there

was a great king named Jahnu of whom the river Gaṅgā became a daughter. The implication clearly is that being the first Āryan king to found a kingdom on the bank of the Gaṅgā, he gave his name to the river which thus became his daughter.

4. *R̥gveda* III, 33, 11-12; 53, 12 & 24. The last verse clearly calls Viśvāmitra and the members of his family *bharatasya putrāḥ,* i.e., descendants of Bharata.
5. *Aitareya Brāhmaṇa* 33, 5.
6. *Śāṅkhāyana Śrauta Sūtra* XV, 25.
7. *Mahābhārata* I, 94; XVIII, 4.
8. IX, 20, 13. The *Padma Purāṇa*, *Svarga Khaṇḍa*, also gives the story, but as its story is clearly borrowed from Kālidāsa's *AbhijñānaŚākuntalam* it has no independent value of its own.
9. *Bhagavadgītā*, XVII.19.
10. *Rāmāyaṇa* I, 50-64; *Mahābhārata* I, 174, 5, etc.
11. It is found only in *Mārkaṇḍeya Purāṇa*, chapters 7 and 8.
12. It is important to remember that Viśvāmitra appears as a contemporary of Rāma only in book I of the *Rāmāyaṇa* which has been proved by Jacobi to be interpolated. He is not at all mentioned in the story of Rāma occurring in the *Mahābhārata* (III, 274-91) and in the *Kūrma Purāṇa* (I, 21). The matter has been fully discussed in Chapter 1.

5

Did Paraśurāma kill his Own Mother?

THREE persons bearing the name Rāma are celebrated in the epics and Purāṇas of India. The first of them was the sage Rāma, son of Jamadagni, the second was king Rāma, son of Daśaratha, and the third was prince Rāma, son of Vasudeva and brother of Kṛṣṇa. Of these, Rāma, son of Jamadagni, was a *ṛṣi* belonging to the early Vedic age and is the reputed author of hymn 110 of the tenth book of the *Ṛgveda*. Having wielded an axe (*paraśu*) for fighting against his adversaries, he is popularly known as Paraśurāma by which appellation we propose to call him.

The most ancient as well as the most illustrious of brāhmaṇa families was that of the Bhārgavas. The earliest *ṛṣis* of this family were Bhṛgu, Dadhīca, Cyavana and Apnavāṇa. Little authentic is known about the first two. Cyavana and Apnavāna are known for their marriages in royal families, for the former married Sukanyā, the daughter of king Śaryāti and the latter married Ruci, the daughter of king Nahuṣa. From Apnavāna was descended a *ṛṣi* named Ūrva. Ūrva's son was Ṛcīka. The latter married Satyavatī, daughter of king Gāthin of Kānyakubja and sister of Viśvāmitra. Ṛcīka's son was the celebrated *ṛṣi* Jamadagni. Vasiṣṭha, Viśvāmitra and the latter's nephew Jamadagni constituted the famous trio of *ṛṣis* in the most glorious epoch of the Ṛgvedic age which saw the rise of three equally renowned monarchs viz., the Haihaya Sahasrabāhu,[1] the Ikṣvāku Hariścandra[2] and the Tṛtsu Sudās.[3] Jamadagni married Reṇukā, a princess of the royal house of Ikṣvākus, and their son was Paraśurāma, greater son of a great father.

Since Paraśurāma's father Jamadagni was, as already stated, a nephew of Viśvāmitra, the account of the birth of Paraśurāma forms a part of the genealogical account of the family of Viśvāmitra which occurs in six of the Purāṇas,[4] in the *Harivaṁśa*[5] and thrice in the *Mahābhārata*.[6] The curious fact that Viśvāmitra, though born in a Kṣatriya family, became a brāhmaṇa and Paraśurāma, though born in a brāhmaṇa family, became virtually a Kṣatriya has been explained by an interesting tale. According to it Satyavatī was given by her husband Ṛcīka two cups of oblation (*caru*), one for herself and the other for her mother, which guaranteed the birth of worthy sons. Satyavatī, however, ate the *caru* meant for her mother and gave the one meant for her to her mother. When Ṛcīka came to know of it he told his wife that she would bear a son possessing the qualities of a Kṣatriya, whereas her mother would give birth to a son, having the qualities of a brāhmaṇa. On Satyavatī's persuasion her husband, however, agreed in her case to transfer the effect of the *caru* from her son to her grandson. In consequence of the *caru* she had eaten Satyavatī's mother gave birth to a son, Viśvāmitra, who became a brāhmaṇa. Satyavatī's son Jamadagni retained his brāhmaṇa qualities, but her grandson Paraśurāma became virtually a Kṣatriya.

It is clear that this story is nothing but an allegory meant for throwing light on the character of two great men of the time viz., Viśvāmitra and Paraśurāma. Viśvāmitra, in contrast with his lineage, was a great spiritual leader, a great poet and a great sage. Paraśurāma on the other hand, though born in a brāhmaṇa family, distinguished himself not as a spiritual leader but as a great warrior who delivered the land from the terror of a tyrant.

The greatest achievement of Paraśurāma which made his name immortal was the killing of the Haihaya king Arjuna Sahasrabāhu, son of Kṛtavīrya, by him. As son of Kṛtavīrya this king was also known as Kārtavīrya by which appellation we propose to call him. The incident of the slaying of Kārtavīrya by Paraśurāma is alluded to in the genealogical account of the Haihayas occurring in nine Purāṇas and *Harivaṁśa*.[7] That Kārtavīrya was a tyrant is proved by the fact that the *Mahābhārata*, the *Harivaṁśa* and five of the Purāṇas[8] inform us that he once set fire to the hermitage of the great *ṛṣi* Vasiṣṭha and was cursed by him. The immediate cause which provoked Paraśurāma to take up arms against him is given in the *Mahābhārata*[9] and the *Bhāgavata*,[10] *Agni*,[11] *Brahmāṇḍa*[12] and *Padma Purāṇa*s. The simplest and the most trustworthy account is found in the *Padma Purāṇa*.[13] According to it the *ṛṣi* Jamadagni had through the favour of Indra obtained a cow that gave excellent and plentiful milk. Once upon a time the Haihaya king Kārtavīrya visited the *ṛṣi* who treated him to dainties prepared from the milk of the cow. Having greatly relished the dishes the king was seized with the desire of taking the cow in his possession, and asked the *ṛṣi* to surrender the cow to him in exchange for a thousand other cows. When the *ṛṣi* resisted the demand of the king, the latter killed him and took away the cow by force. Paraśurāma was away from the hermitage when all this happened. When he returned to the hermitage and saw his father dead he was overpowered with grief and anger and resolved to punish the Haihayas. He attacked the Haihaya kingdom and in the battle that ensued the Haihaya king was killed along with all his allies. At the bidding of his mother, however, he did not harm the Ikṣvākus.

To the account of Paraśurāma given above the *Bhāgavata Purāṇa* and one of the two versions of the *Mahābhārata* (III,116) have added a myth which, briefly told, is as follows. One day when Reṇukā had gone to fetch water from the Gaṅgā she beheld Citraratha, king of the Gandharvas, sporting in the water with his wives. The sight made her envious of their pleasure and she returned defiled by unworthy thoughts. Her husband who could read her thoughts became furious and ordered his sons to cut off her head. The first four sons shrank from the deed but Paraśurāma, the youngest, did not hesitate to obey his father. The deed pacified the father's anger and he desired Paraśurāma to choose a boon. The latter begged that his mother might be restored to life which the father readily granted.

Let us now examine this myth. The first question that naturally occurs to any one making a critical study of the Purāṇas and the great epic is this. Why is it that of all the Purāṇas giving the account of Paraśurāma's deeds the myth occurs only in the *Bhāgavata Purāṇa*? The *Padma Purāṇa* gives the account of Paraśurāma's deeds in greater detail than the *Bhāgavata* and yet it does not give the faintest indication of the slaying of his mother by Paraśurāma at his father's bidding. On the contrary this Purāṇa makes it absolutely clear that Reṇukā was still alive when her husband was killed by the Haihaya king. The *Harivaṁśa* and the *Vāyu, Brahma, Matsya, Linga, Kūrma, Viṣṇu* and *Agni Purāṇa*s similarly are totally ignorant of this myth.[14] So far as the *Mahābhārata* is concerned a similar question arises. Why is it that of the two versions of Paraśurāma's deed occurring in it only one mentions this myth and not the other, although other incidents of the hero's life are mentioned in both the versions? The obvious answer is that the myth must have been invented either by the author who interpolated it in the *Bhāgavata* or by the one who wrote that epic version of the story of Paraśurāma which contains this myth.

It is really immaterial which of the two versions of the myth is earlier. The version occurring in the *Bhāgavata*, however, is clearly grafted, for verses 2-8 of chapter 16 in book IX of this Purāṇa which give this story are totally unconnected with the rest of the matter of this chapter which deals with the assassination of Jamadagni by the sons of Kārtavīrya, the revenge taken by Paraśurāma and the remaining portion of Jahnu's genealogy. Since the genuine matter of this chapter clearly says that Reṇukā survived her husband, the person who grafted the myth of the killing of Reṇukā by Parāśurāma at his father's bidding was compelled to add the miracle of her resurrection. The story found in the *Mahābhārata* was probably borrowed from the *Bhāgavata* and suitably revised, omitting all mention of the survival of Reṇukā after the assassination of her husband. It thus appears that the myth of the killing of his mother by Paraśurāma is the creation of the person who grafted it in the *Bhāgavata Purāṇa* probably with the object of providing an illustration for the virtue of implicit obedience to father. It is a pity that the common man not knowing that the myth does not occur in the account of Paraśurāma's life found in most of the ancient Sanskrit works, has been blindly accepting it for centuries.

Another absurd myth which has clouded the glory of this great hero of ancient India is the one concerning the extermination of Kṣatriyas twenty-one times by him. The credit for this myth also, let it be remembered, goes to the *Mahābhārata* and the *Bhāgavata Purāṇa*. The *Harivaṁśa* and the *Brahma* and *Agni Purāṇas* which do not say a word about it while mentioning Kārtavīrya's death at Paraśurāma's hands in the Haihaya genealogy, stultify themselves when they mention it in a late discourse on the *avatāras* of Viṣṇu.[15] The other *Purāṇas* viz., *Vāyu*, *Matsya*, *Padma*, *Liṅga*, *Kūrma* and *Viṣṇu* which mention Kārtavīrya's death at the hands of Paraśurāma are totally unaware of it.[16] The *Padma Purāṇa* which gives a long account of Paraśurāma's conflict with Kārtavīrya does say that he killed all the kṣatriyas, but not twenty-one times. By all the kṣatriyas the *Padma Purāṇa* no doubt means all the kṣatriyas who were on the side of Kārtavīrya, for it clearly says that Paraśurāma did not quarrel with the Ikṣvākus. The latter therefore must have been on the side of Paraśurāma in his war against the Haihayas. This surmise is fully confirmed by a statement occurring in the *Brahmāṇḍa Purāṇa*[17] according to which only a few generations later the Haihayas attacked Ikṣvāku king Bāhu 'remembering the former hostiliy'. The genuine Purāṇic evidence thus makes it clear that Paraśurāma attacked his enemies only once, that this attack was not directed against all kṣatriyas and that at least one kṣatriya family, that of the Ikṣvākus, was on his side in this attack.

Lastly it should be noted that Paraśurāma was an ancient *ṛṣi* of the Ṛgvedic age. His father Jamadagni has been clearly mentioned in the *Aitareya Brāhmaṇa* as a contemporary of Hariścandra. Yet both the *Rāmāyaṇa*[18] and the *Mahābhārata*[19] have anachronistically made him to suffer defeat in a contest with Rāma and Bhīṣma respectively. The desire of some admirers of Rāma and Bhīṣma to glorify their heroes at the expense of another mighty hero who lived long anterior to both of them is, to say the least, by no means commendable.

References

1. Mentioned in *Ṛgveda* VIII, 45, 26.
2. Mentioned in *Aitareya Brāhmaṇa* 33, 1.
3. Mentioned in *Ṛgveda* VII, etc., and *Aitareya Brāhmaṇa* 35,8; 39, 8.
4. *Vāyu* 91; *Brahmāṇḍa* III,66; *Brahma* 10; *Viṣṇu* IV,7; *Bhāgavata* IX, 15; *Garuḍa* I, 139.
5. *Harivaṁśa* 27.
6. *Mahābhārata* III, 115; XII, 49; XIII, 4.
7. *Vāyu* 94; *Brahmāṇḍa* III, 69; *Brahma* 13; *Mastya* 43; *Padma* V, 12; *Liṅga* I,68; *Kūrma* I, 22; *Viṣṇu* IV, 11; *Agni* 275; *Harivaṁśa* 33.
8. *Mahābhārata* XII, 49. The *Harivaṁśa* and the *Vāyu*, *Brahmāṇḍa*, *Brahma*, *Matsya* and *Padma Purāṇa*s mention this incident in the genealogical account of the Haihayas.
9. *Mahābhārata* III, 116; XII, 49.
10. *Bhāgavata* IX, 15.
11. *Agni* 4, 12-20.
12. *Brahmāṇḍa Purāṇa* III, 21 to 47 (up to verse 63), which mentions the incident of the seizure of Jamadagni's cow by Kārtavīrya in a

long account of the Paraśurāma's deeds, is a very late interpolation, mentioning the cult of Rādhā, and has therefore no historical value.

13. *Padma Purāṇa* VI, 241. It should be remembered that though the different Purāṇas were composed at different times, even the later Purāṇas contain some ancient matter and the older Purāṇas contain some late interpolations. The *Padma Purāṇa*, though one of the later Purāṇas, has preserved some ancient portions here and there and the story of the contest between Paraśurāma and Kārtavīrya in book VI, chapter 241 of this Purāṇa is one of them. This story makes Jamadagni pray to the Vedic god Indra, does not mention the destruction of the kṣatriyas twenty-one times by Paraśurāma and clearly speaks of the latter's lack of hostility towards the Ikṣvākus even in the one war he waged against the kṣatriyas led by Kārtavīrya.

14. The *Brahmāṇḍa Purāṇa* account referred to in footnote 12 above does show its acquiantance with this myth, but as already observed it is a very late interpolation.

15. *Harivaṁśa* 42; *Brahma* 213; *Agni* 4.

16. The late *Brahmāṇḍa Purāṇa* account referred to in footnotes 12 and 14 is aware of this as of other late myths.

17. III, 47, 74.

18. I,73 to 75. Here again it is important to remember that in the story of Rāma occurring in the *Mahābhārata* (III, 274-91), the *Harivaṁśa* (I, 41) and *Brahma* (213), *Kūrma* (I, 21) and *Garuḍa* (143) *Purāṇas* there is no mention of any contest between him and Paraśurāma.

19. V, 178 to 185.

6

Did Bhagīratha bring the Gaṅgā from Heaven?

THE Purāṇic authors have not only denigrated the character of ancient heroes by their myths but have also sometimes obscured their great achievements by mythologizing them. In this category falls the renowned Ikṣvāku king Bhagīratha after whom the river Gaṅgā is known as Bhāgīrathī.

The Ikṣvākus and the Paurava-Bhāratas were the two most illustrious royal dynasties of India in the Vedic period of her history. Many early kings of the Ikṣvāku dynasty are celebrated in both the Vedic literature and the Purāṇas. The most noted of these were Māndhātṛ, Purukutsa, Trasadasyu, Hariścandra and Bhagīratha. The last of these, whose achievements we propose to discuss, is not only mentioned as a famous king in the Ikṣvāku genealogy found in the Purāṇas, but also in the *Jaiminīya Upaniṣad Brāhmaṇa*.

The fame of Bhagīratha rests on the fact that the river Gaṅgā is called Bhāgīrathī after him. According to popular belief, which is based on a myth found in the *Mahābhārata* and the *Bhāgavata Purāṇa*[1] the river received the name Bhāgīrathī because Bhagīratha brought it from heaven. The myth begins with an account of the deeds of Bhagīratha's great-great-grandfather Sagara, whose horse suddenly disappeared when he was performing a horse sacrifice. Sixty thousand of Sagara's soldiers, who are called his sons, went out in search of the horse and found it in the hermitage of a sage named Kapila, but were burnt to ashes when they accused the sage of stealing it. Sagara then sent his gandson Aṁśumat to pacify the sage who told him that the dead persons would obtain salvation only when the celestial river Gaṅgā flowed over their ashes. Aṁśumat therefore performed austerities to bring down the Gaṅgā from heaven but died without achieving success. So did his son Dilīpa. The austerities of Dilīpa's son Bhagīratha at long last pleased the Gaṅgā and she condescended to come down to the earth. She, however, advised Bhagīratha to pray to Śiva to hold her on his head before she descended on the earth, since her terrible velocity would be unbearable if she fell on the earth directly. Bhagīratha then prayed to Śiva who agreed to hold her on his head from where she flowed on the earth.

From myth to history is a far cry. Had this myth been common to all the Purāṇas we could not have helped declaring the connection between Bhagīratha and the river Gaṅgā as unhistorical. A study of the Purāṇas, however, makes it absolutely clear that the myth grew out of very simple facts. Let us examine the matter in some detail.

Besides the *Mahābhārata* and the *Bhāgavata Purāṇa*, ten other Purāṇas and the *Harivaṁśa* explain how the Gaṅgā came to be called Bhāgīrathī. The oldest Purāṇa viz., the *Vāyu* merely says that Bhagīratha brought the Gaṅgā (to light) by his efforts.[2] The *Brahmāṇḍa* follows it but, by misunderstanding the word 'brought' and altering two of the corrupt words occurring in the *Vāyu*, suggests that Gaṅgā was brought to the earth,[3] and the Garuḍa explicitly says so.[4] The *Harivaṁśa* and the *Brahma* and *Agni Purāṇa*s go a step further and say that Bhagīratha caused the Gaṅgā to descend.[5] The *Matsya*, *Padma*, *Liṅga* and *Kūrma Purāṇa*s introduce another innovation by substituting the word *tapas*, austerities, for the earlier *karma*, effort.[6] The *Viṣṇu Purāṇa* brings these changes to their logical conclusion by making Kapila say that the salvation of Sagara's sons depended on the Gaṅgā flowing over their ashes and by attributing to Bhagīratha the feat of bringing the Gaṅgā from the heaven to the earth.[7] This Purāṇa thus prepares the ground for the myth found in the *Bhāgavata Purāṇa* and the *Mahābhārata*.

It is thus clear that a simple statement of fact by the *Vāyu Purāṇa* developed into a fanciful story in the course of some centuries. In order to fully comprehend the achievement of king Bhagīratha it is necessary to cite and explain the complete relevant text of the *Vāyu Purāṇa* which is as follow:

Dilīpāttu mahātejā vīro jāto Bhagīrathaḥ
Yena Gaṅgā saricchreṣṭhā vimānair upaśobhitā
Ījānena samudrād vai duhitṛtvena kalpitā
Atrāpyudāharantīmaṁ ślokaṁ paurāṇikā janāḥ
Bhagīrathas tu tāṁ Gaṅgāmānayāmāsa karmabhiḥ
Tasmād Bhāgīrathī Gaṅgā kathyate vaṁśavittamaiḥ.

Unfortunately the two words '*ījānena samudrāt*' in the beginning of the third line of this passage are corrupt and do not yield any coherent meaning. The *Brahmāṇḍa* has therefore not only substituted new words but has also without any justification changed the case of the first word. The ablative of the second word clearly suggests that the original words indicated the movement of Bhagīratha from some place. If so, the first word must have been '*āyātena*' having come, and not '*ījānena*', having sacrificed. The second word '*samudrāt*', from the sea, has been absurdly changed to '*sureśāt*' from the king of gods, by the *Brahmāṇḍa*. There can be no doubt that the original word was not far removed in sound from the present corrupt word. The only word resembling the present word but yielding a better sense is '*sudūrāt*' meaning 'from afar'. The first two words of the third line were thus in all probability originally '*āyātena sudūrāt*' and were corrupted to '*ījānena samudrāt*'. This emendation is, as we shall see later, supported by the evidence of the *Ṛgveda* as well as the older Purāṇas and certain ancient passages of the *Mahābhārata*.

With this slight emendation the whole passage reads as follows in its English translation:

> From Dilīpa was born the mighty hero Bhagīratha by whom, coming from afar, the excellent river Gaṅgā was adorned with chariots and made into a daughter (i.e. given a name derived from his own). On this subject the Purāṇists cite the following verse. 'Bhagīratha brought the Gaṅgā (to light) by his efforts. Hence the Gaṅgā is called Bhāgīrathī by the experts of dynastic history'.

Any one can see how far removed the account of Bhagīratha's achievement given in this passage of the *Vāyu Purāṇa* is from the later myth found in the *Bhāgavata Purāṇa* and the *Mahābhārata*. There is no mention here of the austerities of Bhagīratha for causing the Gaṅgā to descend from the heaven, of his prayers to Śiva for holding it on his head, of Śiva's gracious compliance, of the river's descent on Śiva's head, and finally of its flowing on the earth from there. Even if we ignore the two corrupt words which we have emended, the main drift of the passage still remains that Bhagīratha brought the Gaṅgā to light, adorned it with chariots and gave it his name. Does it not mean that the Gaṅgā had never before been seen by him, that he came on its bank with numerous chariots carrying his subjects and soldiers and that being the first king of his dynasty to set his foot on its bank he gave it his name? Further, if he was the first king of his dynasty to set his foot on the bank of the Gaṅgā, does it not mean that his ancestors ruled in a region which lay far from the river? Let us see if this conclusion is supported by any independent evidence.

Three of the Purāṇas, viz., the *Vāyu*, the *Brahmāṇḍa* and the *Brahma*, as well as the *Harivaṁśa* and the *Mahābhārata* tell us about a war between the Ikṣvāku king Māndhātṛ and a king of the Druhyu dynasty ruling in Gāndhāra in which the latter was ultimately defeated and killed.[8] This war is said to have lasted for no less than fourteen months according to the unanimous testimony of the *Harivaṁśa* and the *Vāyu, Brahmāṇḍa* and *Brahma Purāṇas*. Common sense tells us that a war in that ancient period could last for such a long time only between neighbours. This long war thus implies that Māndhātṛ was the ruler of a territory situated somewhere in the neighbourhood of Gāndhāra. What is implied in the Purāṇas and the *Mahābhārata* is expressly stated in the *Ṛgveda*. A hymn of it, attributed to Sobhari Kāṇva, praises the gifts which Trasadasyu, a near descendent of Māndhātṛ, conferred on the *ṛṣi* on the bank of the river Suvāstu, the modern Swat.[9] It is thus clear that the Ikṣvākus originally lived in a region to the west of the Indus. There is another interesting piece of evidence in support of this. It is very well-known that the chief rivers of the later Ikṣvāku kindgdom of Kosala were the Gomatī and the Sarayū. The *Ṛgveda* also mentions rivers bearing the names Gomatī and Sarayu but it is certain that they were different from the rivers of Kosala. Gomatī has been identified with a western tributary of the Indus named Gomal. An affluent of the river Gomal is known by the name of Siritoi. It is quite likely that this river is identical with the Ṛgvedic Sarayu. As new places are often given the old names of those very places with which the new-comers had been associated, it is highly probable that the rivers Gomal and Siritoi flowed in the original home of the Ikṣvākus and the two rivers of Kosala were named after them. The ancient kingdom of the Ikṣvākus on the basis of this evidence must have stretched from that river Swat in the north to the rivers Gomal and Siritoi in the south when at its zenith.[10]

It is thus abundantly clear that Bhagīratha did come from afar to the bank of the river Gaṅgā and adorned it with chariots carrying his numerous followers. An ancient heroic laud of the *Mahābhārata*[11] further informs us that he celebrated his arrival on the bank of the holy river by a sacrifice in which he covered it with heaps of gold conferred as gifts on deserving persons. He was, however, not the first Āryan king to settle in the Gangetic region. That honour goes to Jahnu after whom the Gaṅgā was called Jāhnavī. Bhagīratha was, nevertheless, undoubtedly the first Ikṣvāku king to arrive on the bank of the Gaṅgā and therefore felt justified in giving the river his name. He must also have been the founder of the kingdom of Kosala, for according to the *Jaiminīya Upaniṣad Brāhmaṇa*[12] he was a neighbour of and on friendly terms with the Kuru-Pañcālas. Being the founder of a kingdom which was destined to be ruled by a galaxy of illustrious kings and above all by Rāma, Bhagīratha became unforgettable as the discoverer of the chief river of the region where he established the rule of his glorious dynasty.

References

1. *Mahābhārata* III, 107-9; *Bhāgavata* IX, 8-9. The myth also occurs in a much embellished form in Cantos 37 to 43 of the interpolated first book of the *Rāmāyaṇa*.
2. *Vāyu* 88, 167-9.
3. *Brahmāṇḍa* III, 63, 167-9.
4. *Garuḍa* I, 138.
5. *Harivaṁśa* I, 11, 15-16; *Brahma* 8, 75-77; *Agni* 273, 30.
6. *Matsya* 12, 44; *Padma* V, 8, 149-50; *Liṅga* 66, 19-20; *Kūrma* I,21.
7. *Viṣṇu* IV, 4, 35.
8. *Vāyu* 99, 7-8; *Brahmāṇḍa* III, 74, 7-8; *Brahma* 13, 149-50; *Harivaṁśa* I, 32, 124-25; *Mahābhārata* III, 126.
9. *Ṛgveda* VIII, 19, 16-17.
10. The subject of the original home of the Ikṣvākus has been fully discussed by me in the *Journal of the Royal Asiatic Society of Great Britain and Ireland* (No.1, 1976).
11. VII, 60, 1 & 8.
12. IV, 6, I, 2.

7

Did Kṛṣṇa have a Companion named Rādhā?

KṚṢṆA, on the basis of whose teachings was composed the exceedingly charming and highly edifying philosophical poem *Bhagavad Gītā*, was the greatest teacher of the religion now known as Hinduism. Yet, paradoxically, his true character has been completely obscured by the form his worship has taken in the last one thousand years. The earliest mention of Kṛṣṇa, son of Devakī, is found in the *Chāndogya Upaniṣad* where his teacher Ghora Āṅgirasa inculcates the same virtues which are extolled by him in the *Bhagavad Gītā*. The next ancient work which mentions Kṛṣṇa by his patronymic Vāsudeva is the *Aṣṭādhyāyī* of Pāṇini. Megasthenes, the Greek ambassador at the court of Candragupta Maurya, though mentioning him under the name of Herakles, clearly alludes to his name when he mentions the twin cities of Methora (Mathurā) and Kliesobora (Kṛṣṇapura). This Kṛṣṇapura was no doubt another name of Vṛndāvana which might have been so-called because it was here that Kṛṣṇa spent his childhood. The other ancient works where incidental notices of Kṛṣṇa occur are the *Mahābhāṣya* of Patañjali, the Buddhist *Ghaṭa Jātaka* and the Jain *Uttarādhyayana Sūtra*. Three inscriptions viz. those of Besnagar, Ghosundi and Nanaghat prove that Kṛṣṇa had already been deified long before the beginning of the Chiristian era.

Although Kṛṣṇa had no Vālmīki to make him the hero of an

epic, the material found in twelve of the Purāṇas, the *Harivaṁśa* and the *Mahābhārata*[1] relating to the events of his life is no less copious than that found about Rāma in the *Rāmāyaṇa*. Kṛṣṇa, however, had to pay a much heavier penalty for his popularity than Rāma, since the myths, which grew around his genuine life story, are more numerous and extravagant that those which grew around the genuine story of Rāma. Fortunately a collated study of these works enables us to distinguish the genuine from the fake and to reconstruct the correct sequence of events in the life of Kṛṣṇa.

Of the fourteen works which supply information about Kṛṣṇa, the *Mahābhārata* throws light only on the life of the adult Kṛṣṇa, while all the other works deal with his whole life from birth onwards. Four stages are clearly discernible in the growth of the story of the early life of Kṛṣṇa. The earliest account occurs in the *Vāyu* and *Brahmāṇḍa Purāṇa*s and the *Matsya*, *Kūrma*, *Liṅga* and *Garuḍa* follow it. The second stage is discernible in the *Harivaṁśa* and the *Brahma*, *Viṣṇu* and *Agni Purāṇa*s which mention some new incidents in the life of Kṛṣṇa unknown to the earlier six Purāṇas. The third stage is represented by the *Bhāgavata Purāṇa* which mentions certain things for the first time. The *Padma Purāṇa* marks a transition between the third and the fourth stages. Although in its section devoted to the story of Kṛṣṇa the account of the hero's life does not differ from that found in the *Bhāgavata*, it for the first time introduces Rādhā as the companion of Kṛṣṇa in certain other sections. The latest Purāṇa dealing with the life of Kṛṣṇa is the *Brahmvaivarta Purāṇa* which truly represents the fourth stage in the growth of the early life of Kṛṣṇa, for this Purāṇa has for the first time not only introduced Rādhā in the story of Kṛṣṇa but has made her the most prominent figure in his early life. In the later life of Kṛṣṇa there is fortunately no marked disparity between different works dealing with his life.

All the fourteen works which supply information about

Kṛṣṇa are fortunately in agreement about his pedigree. According to the account found in these works Manu Vaivasvata's son Sudyumna was succeeded by the famous king Purūravas whose great-grandson, Yayāti Nāhuṣa, celebrated alike in the *Ṛgveda*, the Purāṇas and the *Mahābhārata*, had five sons, the eldest of whom was Yadu. Yadu's descendants the Yādavas[2] were divided into three branches, the Haihayas, the Vaidarbhas and the Sātvatas. These three branches settled in different regions in course of time. The Sātvatas settled in the Śūrasena regions whose chief city was Mathurā. They branched off into two clans, the Andhakas and the Vṛṣṇis.

A nobleman named Vasudeva, who also bore the appellation of Ānakadundubhi, was born in the Vṛṣṇi subdivision of the Sātvata branch of the Yādavas. Of his many children three survived, viz., the eldest Balarāma or Saṅkarṣaṇa, son of Rohiṇī, and Kṛṣṇa and his younger sister Subhadrā, born of Devakī. Kṛṣṇa was the seventh son of Devakī, the earlier six having been killed by Kaṁsa, the ruler of Mathurā who had usurped the throne after imprisoning his father Ugrasena who happened to be the brother of Devakī's father Devaka. Kaṁsa was thus a cousin of Devakī and was earlier favourably disposed to her, but, relying on a prophecy according to which the seventh son of Devakī was destined to kill him, he wanted to kill Devakī herself. He was, however, persuaded by Vasudeva to spare her on the condition that all children of Vasudeva born of Devakī would be surrendered to him. Kaṁsa then imprisoned Vasudeva and Devakī, who had to surrender their first six sons to him. When the seventh son of Vasudeva and Devakī was born, Vasudeva, having gone to the other side of the Yamunā with the connivance of the prison warders, managed to exchange him with the newly-born daughter of his friend Nanda who lived with his wife Yaśodā in the neighbouring village of Gokula. Vasudeva surrendered the girl to Kaṁsa who killed her. The seventh son of Vasudeva and Devakī thus saved was brought up by his foster-parents Nanda and Yaśodā along with his elder brother who was also left by Vasudeva in the care of Nanda. A few days later Vasudeva secretly sent to Gokula his priest Garga by whom his two sons were given names, the elder being called Balarāma and the younger Kṛṣṇa. They were also given the names of Saṅkarṣaṇa and Keśava respectively. Kṛṣṇa also came to bear the patronymics Vāsudeva, Mādhava and Vārṣṇeya derived from the names of his father Vasudeva and two of his ancestors Madhu and Vṛṣṇi respectively. His great moral qualities earned him the epithets Acyuta (not deviating from righteousness) and Hṛṣīkeśa (having control over senses).

A few years after Kṛṣṇa's birth, Nanda with his family and followers left Gokula on account of an onrush of ferocious wolves and settled in Vṛndāvana. Kṛṣṇa often went in the company of cowherds to tend cows with a cord round his waist whence he got the names Govinda and Dāmodara. His favourite pastime was playing on a flut made of reed whence he got the epithet Muralīdhara.

When Kṛṣṇa was still in his teens, Kaṁsa somehow came to know that the seventh son of Vasudeva and Devakī was safe in Vṛndāvana. He consequently managed to put a mighty bull named Ariṣṭa in the pastures of Vṛndāvana where Kṛṣṇa with his cowherd friends tended the cows. The bull charged at Kṛṣṇa and his friends, but Kṛṣṇa with his muscular body and presence of mind succeeded in killing the beast. Kaṁsa's men then tried to kill Kṛṣṇa by setting a powerful horse named Keśin against him, but Kṛṣṇa, having killed him too, earned the epithet of Keśiniṣūdana.

Realising that discretion was the better part of valour, Kaṁsa sent a Yādava named Akrūra on a peace mission to bring Kṛṣṇa and Balarāma to Mathurā on the pretext of witnessing a grand function being held by Kaṁsa. Akrūra was successful in persuading Kṛṣṇa and Balarāma to accompany him to Mathurā.

When Kṛṣṇa and Balarāma arrived at the court of Kaṁsa, the latter's trained elephant, named Kuvalayāpīḍa, was rushed at them, but the two youths rose to the occasion and killed the beast. Kaṁsa then commissioned his court wrestlers Cāṇūra and Muṣṭika to kill the youths in a wrestling bout, but this time also the tables turned and the wrestlers themselves were killed. Kṛṣṇa then slew the tyrant Kaṁsa himself and reinstated Ugrasena on the throne of Mathurā. Balarāma knew that he was the son of Vasudeva, but Kṛṣṇa had also in the mean time learnt about his real parentage and the two youths were happy to be reunited with their parents.

After the *upanayana* ceremony Kṛṣṇa and Balarāma were sent by Vasudeva to Ujjain to study under the famous scholar, Sāndīpani.[3] On return to Mathurā, Kṛṣṇa had to face the attack of Jarāsandha, the powerful and ambitious king of Magadha (south Bihar), who was enraged at the death of his son-in-law Kaṁsa. Everytime the Magadha monarch was repulsed, he mounted a fresh attack. After facing eighteen invasions the Yādavas on the advice of Kṛṣṇa decided to migrate to what is now Gujarat where they built a stately city named Dvārakā on the sea coast.

Tales of the valourous deeds of Kṛṣṇa reached the ears of Rukmiṇī, daughter of Bhīṣmaka, king of Vidarbha and the desire to marry him arose in her heart. Kṛṣṇa also heard about her beauty and her desire to marry him. He therefore sent a message to her father seeking her hand in marriage. Her brother, Rukmin, however, wanted to marry her to king Śiśupāla of Cedi. To foil the attempt of Rukmin, Kṛṣṇa went to the capital of king Bhīṣmaka and having carried away Rukmiṇī, duly married her.

One of the Yādavas named Satrājit came to possess a radiant gem named Syamantaka. He went through the streets of Dvārakā with that gem on his person and while everyone felt dazzled, Kṛṣṇa admiringly said that he wished he could have a gem like that. Soon after that Satrājit gave that gem to his brother Prasena, who, while he was on a hunting expedition, with the gem on his person, was killed by a lion. A certain Jāmbavat, who is wrongly identified by some of the Purāṇas with the Jāmbavat of Rāma's time, took off that gem from the body of Prasena and went home with it. In the meantime Satrājit and the other Yādavas began to suspect Kṛṣṇa's hand in the death of Prasena. To vindicate his honour Kṛṣṇa went in search of Prasena. Following the marks of the hoofs of the horse on whose back Prasena had gone out hunting, he reached the abode of Jāmvabat. There was a duel between him and Jāmbavat and the latter, having acknowledge defeat, gave him his daughter Jāmbavatī in marriage along with that gem.

Kṛṣṇa returned to Dvārakā and gave the gem back to Satrājit. The latter felt ashamed for his false suspicion against Kṛṣṇa and to make amends for it offered him the hand of his daughter Satyabhāmā. Kṛṣṇa accepted the proposal and married Satyabhāmā. Another Yādava named Śatadhanvan who had wanted to marry Satyabhāmā felt so enraged that he secretly killed Satrājit and took possession of the gem. When Satyabhāmā came to know of her father's death at the hands of Śatadhanvan she was beside with grief. Kṛṣṇa in the meantime had gone to Vāraṇāvata on hearing about the Pāṇḍavas' supposed death in the wax house build by Duryodhana. Satyabhāmā rushed to inform her husband about the tragedy and Kṛṣṇa, having promised to avenge her father's death, came back to Dvārakā.

When Śatadhanvan learnt about Kṛṣṇa's arrival he was so frightened that he gave the gem to Akrūra and fled away in a chariot. Kṛṣṇa and Balarāma chased him and when they were about to overtake him, he jumped from his chariot and ran to save his life. Kṛṣṇa left Balarāma in the chariot and running after the fleeing Śatadhanvan caught him and despatched him off. He was, however, sorry when he did not find the gem in the possession of the slain Śatadhanvan. Kṛṣṇa came back and reported the matter to Balarāma who, however, doubting the truth of Kṛṣṇa's statement, refused to go back to Dvārakā with him. Kṛṣṇa, sad and helpless, went back alone to Dvārakā. Later, on the persuasion of the Yādavas, Balarāma too returned to Dvārakā.

In the meantime Akrūra was performing numerous sacrifices which led Kṛṣṇa to suspect that the former was probably in the possession of the lost gem. When the Yādavas met in an assembly Kṛṣṇa expressed his suspicion to Akrūra and asked him to produce the gem. Akrūra confessed the truth and placed the gem before Kṛṣṇa and the other Yādavas. Since Satyabhāmā was the only surviving issue of Satrājit, she and her husband Kṛṣṇa were the real claimants of the gem. Kṛṣṇa, however, generously allowed Akrūra to keep the gem with him, and thus ended the episode of the Syamantaka gem.

Naraka, king of Prāgjyotiṣapura in what is now Assam, was a great tyrant and the news of his atrocities reached the ears of Kṛṣṇa. Having resolved to liberate the people from his stranglehold, Kṛṣṇa marched against him. At the gate of the city he was challenged by Naraka's general Mura. Kṛṣṇa killed him after a heroic fight and thus earned the epithet Murāri. He then entered the city where Naraka met him with his army. A battle took place in which Naraka was worsted and killed.

The Pāṇḍavas being the cousins of Kṛṣṇa, he had very friendly relations with them and specially with Arjuna, the third Pāṇḍava prince, to whome his sister Subhadrā was married. Bhīma, the second Pāṇḍava prince, was successful in killing Jarāsandha, king of Magadha, under Kṛṣṇa's directions. The Pāṇḍavas having made their kingdom secure, Yudhiṣṭhira, the eldest Pāṇḍava and the ruler of the kingdom, decided to perform a *rājasūya* sacrifice. The real greatness of Kṛṣṇa was revealed on the occasion of this sacrifice. When the duties pertaining to that sacrifice were divided among the close associates of Yudhiṣṭhira, Kṛṣṇa of his own sweet will chose the work of washing the feet of worthy brāhmaṇas. When the sacrifice started the assembled guests had to be honoured and according to the protocol of those times the worthiest guest had to be given precedence over all others. Kṛṣṇa was declared as the worthiest guest by the consensus of the assembly notwithstanding the fact that there were persons present who were either more aged than the Yādava hero or possessed much greater wealth and prestige as rulers of mighty kingdoms. The honour bestowed on Kṛṣṇa enraged Śiśupāla, king of Cedi (modern Bundelkhand), who heaped vile abuses upon him. Kṛṣṇa calmly ignored the fulminations of Śiśupāla but when the latter challenged him to fight he accepted the challenge and in the encounter that followed, the Cedi monarch was killed.

A friend of Śiśupāla was the king of Śālva (the region around Alwar in Rajasthan). When he heard of the death of Śiśupāla at the hands of Kṛṣṇa, he, taking advantage of the Yādava leader's absence from Dvārakā, attacked the city. Kṛṣṇa, however, came to know of the Śālva king's treacherous act in time and rushed to Dvārakā. In the battle that followed Kṛṣṇa defeated and killed the Śālva king.

The kingdom of Puṇḍra in what is now West Bengal was ruled in Kṛṣṇa's time by a king who bore the same patronymic as Kṛṣṇa viz., Vāsudeva. The fame of Kṛṣṇa Vāsudeva having reached his ears he proclaimed that he was the Vāsudeva who had won fame by his great achievements and not Kṛṣṇa. He even committed the folly of sending a messenger to Kṛṣṇa asking him to give up the name Vāsudeva. Kṛṣṇa therefore resolved to teach him a lesson. He attacked the Puṇḍra king and killed him along with his ally, the king of Kāśī.

With the destruction of the kings of Cedi, Śālva and Puṇḍra a good number of swollen-headed monarchs of the time of Kṛṣṇa were liquidated. Dantavakra, king of Karūṣa (the region round the modern Rewa), however, refused to learn a lesson. Hoping to avenge the defeat of his friends he attacked Dvārakā. Kṛṣṇa, invincible as ever, vanquished the assailant, who was killed along with his brother.

The Sātvata Yādavas formed a republican corporation and their Sanghamukhya or Elder of the confederacy was for a long time Ugrasena. Kṛṣṇa in course of time became extremely popular. The Yādavas eventually elected him their Sanghamukhya and he retained that position till the end of his life.

As the penalty for losing at dice against Duryodhana, the Pāṇḍavas were banished for thirteen years. At the end of that period they re-claimed their principality. Kṛṣṇa acted as their emissary of peace to Duryodhana and tried his best to persuade the latter to give only five villages to the Pāṇḍavas but Duryodhana refused to part even with as much land as would be covered by the tip of a needle. Notwithstanding his stubbornness, Duryodhana invited Kṛṣṇa to a royal banquet, but the latter, with his characteristic love for the humble, spurned the delicacies to which Duryodhana wanted to treat him and preferred an austere meal at the house of Vidura.

Kṛṣṇa's efforts at reconciliation having proved futile, the Pāṇḍavas appealed to arms. In the great Bhārata battle that took place on the field of Kurukṣetra, Kṛṣṇa offered his personal help to the Pāṇḍava prince Arjuna as his charioteer. Kṛṣṇa was not only a great warrior but also a great teacher and his sermon to Arjuna on the battle-field before the contest actually started has been immortalized under the name of *Bhagavad Gītā*[4] by the poet of the *Mahābhārata*. During this great war Kṛṣṇa helped and guided the Pāṇḍavas a number of times and the victory of the latter was in a very large measure due to him.

Kṛṣṇa returned to Dvārakā after Yudhiṣṭhira was crowned at Hastināpura. He had a number of children, the most noted being his sons Pradyumna and Sāmba born of Rukmiṇi and Jāmbavatī respectively. Pradyumna's son was the famous Aniruddha. Some years after the Bhārata war the Yādavas were ruined by fratricidal strife and as Kṛṣṇa sat brooding under a tree, an arrow discharged by a hunter accidentally struck his heel. The hunter was shocked when he found that his arrow had hit the great Yādava leader, but Kṛṣṇa consoled him and left for his heavenly abode. The remnants of the Yādava family abandoned Dvārakā on which the sea had encroached and retreated northwards under Arjuna's leadership but were attacked and broken up by the Ābhīras (Ahirs) dwelling in what is now Rajasthan. Arjuna took the surviving Yādavas to Indraprastha and placed Kṛṣṇa's great-grandson Vajra as king over them.

The above narrative of Kṛṣṇa's life contains only such information as is common to all the Purāṇas and is found in what appear to be the ancient portions of the *Mahābhārata*. It may, therefore, be reasonably regarded as genuine.

With the growth of the number and contents of the Purāṇas in later times the great Yādava warrior and teacher had to pay a heavy penalty for his popularity. The priests who took charge of the Purāṇas went on adding new features to the life of Kṛṣṇa, in order to justify their own corrupt practices. The growth of the story of Kṛṣṇa affords a glaring example where we can detect the stages by which history is gradually turned into mythology.

The earliest feature added to the original life story of Kṛṣṇa was the latter's marriage with 16100 maidens who are said to have been freed from the captivity of Naraka, king of Prāgjyotiṣapura, when the latter was killed. Though this incident is mentioned in all the Purāṇas, it is conspicuous by its absence in the deeds of Kṛṣṇa mentioned in *Mahābhārata,* V,48. This chapter of the *Mahābhārata* describes the battle between Kṛṣṇa and Naraka in as many as eight verses. Yet there is not the slightest hint about these maidens. Had the author of this account of Kṛṣṇa's deeds known about the incident of his releasing and marrying the maidens imprisoned by Naraka, he could not have failed to mention it. It was clearly invented at a date later than that of the *Mahābhārata* account of Kṛṣṇa's deeds.

The author of the *Viṣṇu Purāṇa* has, in his anxiety to make this incident appear genuine, even committed the fault of anachronism. In the episode of the Syamantaka gem this Purāṇa has made Kṛṣṇa to say that he did not deserve to keep the gem with him because he had over sixteen thousand wives. But according to this Purāṇa itself, in agreement with the other Purāṇas dealing with the story of Kṛṣṇa, the latter killed Naraka and married 16100 damsels long after the Syamantaka episode because Satyabhāmā whom he married after returning the gem to her father was with him when he attacked and killed Naraka. He, therefore, could not have said what the Purāṇa puts in his mouth.

We now come to the other features added to the story of Kṛṣṇa from time to time. The earlier Purāṇas viz., the *Vāyu, Brahmāṇḍa, Matsya, Kūrma, Liṅga* and *Garuḍa* regard Kṛṣṇa as the seventh son of Devakī. The later Purāṇas on the other hand regard Balarāma as the seventh son of Devakī and have coined the myth that he was transferred from her womb to that of Rohiṇī. Kṛṣṇa was thus according to them the eighth son of Devakī.[5] It is clear that the version of the older Purāṇas is correct.

The later Purāṇas, *Brahma, Viṣṇu, Agni, Bhāgavata* and *Padma* as well as the *Harivaṁśa* mention some tales about Kṛṣṇa which are altogether unknown to the earlier Purāṇas. The taming of the serpent Kāliya, the worship and lifting of Govardhana and the performance of *rāsa* or *hallīśa* dance by Kṛṣṇa which occur in the later Purāṇas do not find any mention in the earlier ones and were therefore undoubtedly the creation of the authors of the later Purāṇas. The killing of Kaṁsa's washerman and the curing of the deformity of his hunch-back maidservant by Kṛṣṇa are similarly mentioned in the later Purāṇas only and cannot therefore be regarded as genuine. The story of Kṛṣṇa's breaking the bow at the court of Kaṁsa which also occurs only in the later Purāṇas was clearly coined in imitations of Rāma's feat in the *Rāmāyaṇa*.

Of the Purāṇas dealing with the life story of Kṛṣṇa one of the latest is the *Bhāgavata*. This Purāṇa mentions some incidents which are totally unknown even ot those later Purāṇas which were composed earlier than it. The most well-known of these incidents is the seizing of the clothes of the cowherdesses by Kṛṣṇa when they were bathing in the Yamunā.[6] The authors of the *Harivaṁśa* and the *Brahma, Viṣṇu* and *Agni Purāṇa*s, which give a detailed account of the deeds of Kṛṣṇa could not have failed to mention this event if it was known to them. Since it is not mentioned in these works it is clearly the creation of the author of the *Bhāgavata Purāṇa*.

We now pass on to the latest but the most significant addition made to the story of Kṛṣṇa, viz., the introduction of the cowherdess Rādhā in his early life at Gokula and Vṛndāvana. Since the *Mahābhārata* gives glimpses only of his later life we cannot expect it to mention the name of Rādhā. What is, however, most amazing is the fact that the person today most closely associated with Kṛṣṇa is totally unknown not only to the ancient *Vāyu, Matsya, Kūrma, Liṅga* and *Garuḍa Purāṇa*s which give a brief account of his early life but also to the *Harivaṁśa* and the *Brahma, Viṣṇu, Agni* and *Bhāgavata Purāṇa*s which give a detailed account of his early life.[7] The *Brahmāṇḍa Purāṇa* too, like its counterpart *Vāyu*, does not mention Rādhā in its account of Kṛṣṇa. Her name occurs in it only in a portion describing the adventures of Paraśurāma which was interpolated in it at a very late period. Even the late *Padma Purāṇa* does not mention Rādhā in its original story of Kṛṣṇa occurring in the *Uttara khaṇḍa*. Her name occurs only in its late *Brahma* and *Pātāla khaṇḍa*s in myths and descriptions of rituals unconnected with the life story of the great Yādava hero.

It is only the latest of the Purāṇas giving an account of Kṛṣṇa's life, viz., the *Brahmavaivarta* which introduces Rādhā in the account of his life and that too in a totally incredible manner. This Purāṇa contains four sections, viz., *Brahma khaṇḍa*, *Prakṛti khaṇḍa*, *Gaṇapati khaṇḍa* and *Śrī Kṛṣṇa Janma khaṇḍa*. The last *khaṇḍa*, as its name indicates, deals with the life of Kṛṣṇa. The account of Rādhā, however, first occurs in chapter 40 of the second section according to which she was the wife of Yaśodā's brother Rāyaṇa and was thus Kṛṣṇa's aunt and much older in age than him. The Purāṇa then temporarily takes leave of her until in chapter 66 of the last section dealing with Kṛṣṇa's life she is again introduced in an absurd story which is as follows.

Once when Nanda had taken his cows to the pastures of Vṛndāvana with the infant Kṛṣṇa in his lap, it bagan to rain in torrents. Kṛṣṇa began to cry as he heard the thundering of clouds and this made Nanda panicky. Just at that moment Rādhā came there. Nanda bowed to her and, having observed that he knew both her and his son Kṛṣṇa to be none other than Lakṣmī and Viṣṇu respectively, handed over Kṛṣṇa to her. Rādhā took Kṛṣṇa to a place where stood a charming canopy studded with precious stones. On reaching there the infant Kṛṣṇa miraculously turned into a handsome young man and reminded Rādhā that she was none other than his Śakti. As soon as Kṛṣṇa spoke these words, Brahmā, the creator of the world, himself arrived there and, acting as a priest, solemnized the marriage of Kṛṣṇa with Rādhā.[8] Soon after the marriage had been solemnized Brahmā went beck to his heaven and Kṛṣṇa again becam a child. Rādhā then took him to Vṛndāvana and handed him over to his mother Yaśodā.

It is clear, as any intelligent person can see, that the account of Rādhā contained in this Purāṇa is full of absurdities. Even if this account of Rādhā were to be found in all the Purāṇas, she could not have been regarded as a historical person. Since, however, she is totally unknown to all of the earlier Purāṇas dealing with the life of Kṛṣṇa, her mythical origin is proved beyond a shadow of doubt. It is a shame that a corrupt priesthood played havoc with the life of a truly great man. It is a greater shame that the Hindu became a willing victim of the wiliness of this priesthood.

References

1. *Vāyu* 96 and 98 (94-104); *Brahmāṇḍa* III,71 and 73 (94-103); *Matsya* 45-47; *Kūrma* I, 24; Liṅga 2, 69; *Garuḍa* I, 139; *Brahma* 180-212; *Viṣṇu* IV, 13-15 and V; *Agni* 12 and 275-6; *Bhāgavata* IX, 24 and X; *Padma* VI, 245-252; *Brahmavaivarta* IV; *Harivaṁśa* I, 34-39 and II; *Mahābhārata* II, 33-45; V 48, etc.
2. The Bhāṭī Rājpūts of Jaisalmer claim to be the descendants of the ancient Yādavas.
3. According to the *Chāndogya Upaniṣad* Kṛṣṇa's teacher was Ghora Āṅgirasa. Thus either Kṛṣṇa studied under two teachers or Ghora was the personal name of Sāndīpani which was a patronymic meaning son of Sandīpana.
4. The original *Bhagavad Gītā* contained only the first six and the last six of its present eighteen chapters as shown by me in my two articles entitled "Additions and Interpolations in the Bhagavad Gītā" published in *East and West*, Rome, Italy (Dec. 1977) and "Names and Epithets of Kṛṣṇa in the Bhagavad Gītā" published in *Indologica Taurinensia,* Turin, Italy (Vol. VII, 1979).
5. The poet Bhāsa, though following the *Harivaṁśa* and the later Purāṇas in mentioning the exploits of Kṛṣṇa in his *Bālacarita*, calls the hero of his play the seventh son of Devakī in accordance with the older Purāṇas at which Keith, familiar only with the later Purāṇas, expresses surprise in his *Sanskrit Drama*, p. 98.
6. *Bhāgavata* X, 22.
7. She is unknown to the poet Bhāsa also who wrote the play *Bālacarita* to celebrate the early life of Kṛṣṇa.
8. It is difficult to understand how Brahmā condescended to soleminze the marriage of Kṛṣṇa with Rādhā, when she was already married to Rāyaṇa.

8

Was Yudhiṣṭhira Crowned King of Hastināpura in 3102 BC?

THREE great events, the Bhārata war, the coronation of Yudhiṣṭhira as king of Hastināpura and the birth of Parikṣit II took place in quick succession within the same year. If we can approximately fix the date of any one of these events, the date of the other two is automatically established. We may, therefore, take up the date of the coronation of Yudiṣṭhira for discussion.

According to the testimony of the celebrated astronomer Āryabhaṭa (AD 499) and that of the Aihole inscription of Ravikīrti (AD 634) the coronation of Yudhiṣṭhira took place in 3102 BC. This date is, however, totally inconsistent with the evidence supplied by the Purāṇic genealogies according to which only 34 generations ruled between the coronation of Yudhiṣṭhira and the coronation of Candragupta Maurya which is known to have taken place around 320 BC. If we accept 3102 BC as the date of Yudhiṣṭhira's coronation it will mean that the average reign period of kings who ruled between Yudhiṣṭhira and Candragupta Maurya was about 82 years which is impossible.[1] This date therefore must be rejected.

Another tradition which mentions the period of interval between the birth of Parikṣit and the coronation of Mahāpadma Nanda is recorded by the compilers of the Purāṇas. According to this tradition a period of 1050 years elapsed between the two events. Since, however, there were two kings of the name of Parikṣit in the dynasty to which Yudhiṣṭhira belonged and since the Purāṇas do not make it clear as to which Parikṣit is meant, this tradition is of no value in determining the date of the coronation of Yudhiṣṭhira.[2]

The period lying between the coronation of Yudiṣṭhira and the coronation of Candragupta Maurya may conveniently be divided into two eras viz, (1) the pre-Buddha era, and (2) the post-Buddha era. Fortunately we have enough material at our disposal for determining the chronology of the post-Buddha era. As the best way of historical investigation is to proceed from the better known to the less known, we shall first determine the names, order and chronology of the kings of the post-Buddha era and then take up the kings of the pre-Buddha era for arriving at an appoximate date of the coronotion of Yudhiṣṭhira.

The earliest serious study of the history of the post-Buddha era as recorded in the Purāṇas was done by the late F.E. Pargiter whose monumental work on the subject entitled *The Purāṇa Text of the Dynasties of the Kali Age* is still the most valuable reference book on the subject. Since then much work has been done on the history of the period following the birth of Buddha and preceding the foundation of the Maurya empire, but many problems continue to remain unresolved. The order of kings in the Purāṇic lists is in several cases different from that found in other works both Brāhmaṇical and Buddhist. Similarly, the regnal years of kings as given in the Purāṇas are different from those given in the Buddhist chronicle *Mahāvaṁsa* of Sri Lanka. These problems are, however, not really insoluble for, as we shall see, we can reconstruct a correct history of the post-Buddha era by using the material found in the Purāṇas.

Before proceeding to test the veracity of the account given in the Purāṇas it is necessary to reiterate four very important things concerning the Purāṇa text which were pointed out by Pargiter:

1. There are some clear misplacements which, as rightly pointed out by Pargiter, have occurred through the carelessness of the copyists. Thus the *Matsya Purāṇa* has introduced the first two Kāṇvāyana kings after Bimbisāra and consequently made changes in the verse mentioning the total number of kings. Similarly the *Vāyu Purāṇa* has wrongly placed Ajātaśatru two steps before Bimbisāra. It, therefore, follows that if there is unimpeachable evidence about the wrong position of some kings in the Purāṇic list we have a right to put the verse or hemistich mentioning that king in its proper place.

2. There is often great variation in names. As pointed out by Pargiter, in some cases the correct form can be selected by reference to other books or inscriptions.

3. As regards regnal years, the names of some of the numbers being very much alike, the copyists have often mistaken one for the other. These numbers are *viṁśat* and *triṁśat*, *caturviṁśat* and *catvāriṁśat*. Since the first number of each of these two pairs is not grammatically quite correct,[3] it is generally the first that has been substituted by the second and not *vice versa*, so that wherever both of a pair occur in different manuscripts the first may be selected, unless there is some cogent evidence in favour of the second. Even when all the manuscripts give only one number out of any of these pairs, the other of the pair may be selected if there are convincing reasons for doing so.

4. As pointed out by Pargiter, the correct form of a word in the Purāṇa text is sometimes what would appear to be an aberrant form.

We now come to the Purāṇa text of the four powerful dynasties that ruled in Avantī and Magadha after the birth of Buddha and before the accession of Candragupta Maurya. These four dynasties were the Pradyotas, the Kṣemadharmajas, the Śiśunāgas and the Nandas. The first two of these ruled contemporaneously in Avantī and Magadha respectively and they were succeeded in turn by the Śiśunāgas and the Nandas. We begin with the Pradyota dynasty which is mentioned first by all the Purāṇas.

There is as usual great variation in the names of the kings of the Pradyota dynasty. As pointed out by Professor Rapson,[4] the correct form of the name of the father of the first king Pradyota, which is variously mentioned as Pulika and Śunika, was Puṇika on the authority of Bāṇa's *Harsacarita*. The king who is variously mentioned as Sūryaka and Ajaka in the Purāṇas was really Āryaka as we learn from the ancient play *Mṛcchakaṭikam*. Āryaka in Prākṛta would be Ajjaka which could easily become Ajaka, and by the change of the first syllable it became Sūryaka. The correct name of the last king, who is variously called as Nandivardhana and Vartivardhana was undoubtedly Avantivardhana.

So far as the order of these kings is concerned there is one clear misplacement. The play *Mṛcchakaṭikam* makes it absolutely clear that king Pālaka, son of Pradyota, was succeeded by Āryaka. In placing Viśākhayūpa between Pālaka and Āryaka, the copyists of the Purāṇas have no doubt mistakenly interchanged the places of the hemistichs mentioning Āryaka and Viśākhayūpa.

As regards regnal years of these kings, they appear to be quite correct since their total agrees with the period of 138 years assigned to the dynasty. The other figure of 52 years is clearly wrong.

With these corrections the account of Pradyotas would read as follows:

बृहद्रथेष्वतीतेषु नीतिहोत्रेष्ववन्तिषु ।
पुणिकःस्वामिनं हत्वा स्वपुत्रमभिषेक्ष्यति ।।

मिषतां क्षत्रियाणां हि प्रथोतं पुणिको बलात् ।
स वै प्रणतसामन्तो भविष्यो नयवर्जितः ।।

त्रयोविंशत्समा राजा भविता स नरोत्तमः ।
चतुर्विंशत्समा राजा पालको भविता ततः ।।

एकविंशत्समा राज्यमार्यकस्य भविष्यति ।
विशाखयूपो भविता नृपः पंचाशतीं समाः ।।

भविष्यति समा विंशत्तत्सुतोऽवन्तिवर्धनः ।
अष्टत्रिंशच्छतं भाव्याः प्रद्योताः पंच ते नृपाः ।।

We now pass on to the kings whom the Purāṇas in their present form treat as belonging to the dynasty of Śiśunāga. So fas as the names of these kings are concerned, despite great variation, there is no dispute in the case of most of them whose true forms are known from other sources. Only two of the names present some difficulty. The name of Kṣemadharman also occurs as Kṣemavarman, but the former is the more common form which may therefore be accepted as correct. His son is similarly given two different names Kṣatraujas and Kṣemajit. The former, being more common, may be accepted as the true name.

When we take up the question of the order of kings in this list we cannot have any doubt that the first two verses giving the account of the reigns of Śiśunāga and his son Kākavarṇa have been misplaced. In this connection the first thing to be noted is that all ancient works, whether Brāhmaṇical or Buddhist, which refer to the history of this period, make it absolutely clear that kings Bimbisāra and Ajātaśatru of this list were contemporaries of Pradyota, the founder of the ruling dynasty of Avantī mentioned earlier. Thus according to the *Majjhima Nikāya* Ajātaśatru fortified his capital Rājagṛha[5] in anticipation of an attack by Pradyota of Avantī. The *Svapnavāsavadattam* of Bhāsa, likewise makes Pradyota and his son Pālaka of Avantī as well as the Magadhan king Darśaka, son of Ajātaśatru, contemporaries of the hero of the play, king Udayana of Vatsa. Pradyota was succeeded by four kings in turn and so was Ajātaśatru, his Magadhan contemporary. The two dynasties must have, therefore, ended about the same time. The question naturally arises as to who succeeded them. The Buddhist chronicles of Sri Lanka are not the only works which regard Śiśunāga and his son as having ruled over Magadha after the destruction of the dynasty of Bimbisāra. The north Indian Divyāvadāna too regards Kākavarṇin, and therefore impliedly his father Śiśunāga, as having followed the last descendant of Bimbisāra. The Purāṇas themselves place Śiśunāga after the Pradyotas and when they say that he placed his son in Vārāṇasī and made Girivraja his own abode they unknowingly indicate that he could not have preceded Bimbisāra. Since the region of Kāśī whose chief city was Vārāṇasī did not form part of the Magadhan kingdom before the time of Bimbisāra, Śiśunāga could not have placed his son in Vārāṇasī if he had preceded Bimbisāra. Similarly when the Purāṇas say that Śiśunāga made Girivraja his abode they imply that it had ceased to be the capital of Magadha when Śiśunāga founded his dynasty and he restored it to its ancient position for a while. This also proves that he came long after Bimbisāra, for Girivraja continued to be the capital of Magadha till the time of Udāyin who built Pāṭaliputra, the new capital of Magadha. All available evidence thus indisputably points to the fact that the first two verses of this list must come after the hemistich which follows the one mentioning king Mahānandin and sums up the account of the dynasty of Kṣemadharman. It is clear that the last word of this hemistich as found in the *Matsya Purāṇa* was originally 'Kṣemadharmataḥ' and was changed to 'Śiśunāgataḥ' when the verses giving the account of the Śiśunāga dynasty were misplaced.[6]

We now take up the regnal years of these kings. The reign period of king Kṣemadharman is given as *viṁśati* (20) by the *Vāyu* and *Brahmāṇḍa Purāṇa*s and *ṣaṭ-triṁśat* (36) by some copies of the *Mastya*, while the copy called *n Matsya* by Pargiter gives the figure *ṣaḍiṁśati*, i.e., *ṣaḍviṁśati* (26). It seems that the correct number is 26 because it alone could be changed to 36 in one set of Purāṇas and 20 in another set. The next king Kṣatraujas is assigned *catvāriṁśat* (40) years by the *Vāyu* and *Brahmāṇḍa* and *caturviṁśat* (24) by *Matsya*. Here the correct figure is no doubt 24. The better readings in the cases of Bimbisāra, Ajātaśatru and Darśaka are 28, 25 and 24 years respectively. Udāyin is unanimously assigned a period of 33 years by all the Purāṇas. The best reading of the reign periods of the last two kings, Nandivardhana and Mahānandin is found in the *n* Matsya which is as follows:

> *catvāriṁśat samā bhāvyo rājā vai Nandivardhanaḥ.*
> *catvāriṁśat tataś caiva mahānandībhaviṣyati.*

One very pertinent observation must be made here. It is highly improbable that after Udāyin's long reign of 33 years his two successors reigned for the longer period of 40 years each. As observed earlier, copyists have often substituted *catvāriṁśat* (40) for *caturviṁśat* (24). In some cases as in that of Kṣatraujas both the readings have been preserved, while in others the original figure was totally discarded. We have thus good reason to suspect that the figure *catvāriṁśat* in the case of these two kings was originally *caturviṁśat*.

As for the regnal years of the Śiśunāgas, the first king, Śiśunāga, is unanimously assigned 40 years by all the Purāṇas. His son is assigned 26 years by Matsya and 36 years by *Vāyu* and *Brahmāṇḍa*. There can be no doubt that the correct figure is 26. The last verse in this account gives the total period of the Śiśunāga dynasty. The figure given in most of the Purāṇas is 360 or 362 years either of which is impossible. Here an aberrant reading comes to our rescue, and must undoubtedly have been the correct original reading. The *bVāyu* has the reading *'etāni'* in place of *'śatāni'*. The meaning of the hemistich thus becomes "these three and sixty-two years" in place of "three hundred and sixty-two years". This reading agrees with the aggregate of the reigns of the two Śiśunāga kings.[7]

With these corrections the account of the Kṣemadharmajas and Śiśunāgas would read as follows:

षड्विंशतिं च वर्षाणि क्षेमधर्मा भविष्यति ।
चतुर्विंशत्समा राज्यं क्षत्रौजाः प्राप्स्यते ततः ।।

अष्टाविंशति वर्षाणि बिम्बिसारो भविष्यति ।
अजातशत्रुर्भविता पंचविंशत्समा नृपः ।।

चतुर्विंशत्समा राजा दर्शकस्तु भविष्यति ।
उदायी भविता तस्मात् त्रयस्त्रिंशत्समा नृपः ।।

स वै पुरवरं राजा पृथिव्यां कुसुमाह् वयम् ।
गंगाया दक्षिणे कूले चतुर्गेऽब्दे करिष्यति ।।

चतुर्विंशत्समा भाव्यो राजा वै नन्दिवर्धनः ।
चतुर्विंशत्ततश्चैव महानन्दी भविष्यति ।।

इत्येते भवितारोऽत्र वंशे वै क्षेमधर्मतः ।
हत्वा तेषां यशः कृत्स्नं शिशुनागो भविष्यति ।।

वाराणस्यां सुतं स्थाप्य श्रयिष्यति गिरिब्रजम् ।
शिशुनागश्च वर्षाणि चत्वारिंशद्भविष्यति ।।

काकवर्णः सुतस्तस्य षड्विंशत् प्राप्स्यते महीम् ।

एतानि त्रीनि वर्षाणि द्विषष्ट्यभ्यधिकानि तु ।
शिशुनागा भविष्यन्ति राजानः क्षत्र बन्धवः ।।[8]

The last of the pre-Mauryan dynasties, that of the Nandas, does not present much difficulty. Mahāpadma was the name of the founder of this dynasty according to the unanimous testimony of the Purāṇas. He was the son of Mahānandin and so must have been at least 65 years of age when he wrested Magadha from Kākavarṇa Śaiśunāgi. He was succeeded by his eight sons, the name of only the eldest of whom is mentioned as Sukalpa or Sumālya. The reign period of Mahāpadma is given as 28 years in most *Vāyu* manuscripts and 88 in other Purāṇas.[9] There can be no doubt that the correct reading is 28. His eight sons who ruled simultaneously are unanimously assigned 12 years.

The Purāṇic list of kings of the four pre-Mauryan dynasties with their regnal years are thus as follows:

Pradyotas

Pradyota	reigned	23 years	Total 138 years
Pālaka	reigned	24 years	
Aryaka	reigned	21 years	
Viśākhayūpa	reigned	50 years	
Avantivardhana	reigned	20 years	

Kṣemadharmajas

Kṣemadharman	reigned	26 years	Total 208 years
Kṣatraujas	reigned	24 years	
Bimbisāra	reigned	28 years	
Ajātaśatru	reigned	25 years	
Darśaka	reigned	24 years	
Udāyin	reigned	33 years	
Nandivardhana	reigned	24 years	
Mahānandin	reigned	24 years	

Śiśunāgas

Śiśunāga	reigned	about 40 years	Total 65 years
Kākavarṇa	reigned	about 26 years	

Nandas

Mahāpadma	reigned	28 years	Total 40 years
His eight sons	reigned	12 years	

This account of pre-Mauryan dynasties as found in the Purāṇas can be regarded as credible only if it is found to be in accord with the dates of some events known from other sources. According to Sri Lankan tradition the *nirvāṇa* of Buddha occurred in 544 BC, when king Ajātaśatru, son of Bimbisāra, had been reigning eight years. The date of the *nirvāṇa* of Buddha has been a subject of keen controversy and scholars have been vascillating between 544 BC, the Sri Lankan date of the Great Decease and 486 BC, the starting point of the dotted record found at the Chinese city of Canton. There are, however, two important considerations which go in favour of the Sri Lankan date. In the first place, as observed by Max Müller long ago, the process of adding one dot at the end of every year during so long a time as 975 years was extremely precarious. Secondly the Cantonese date goes against the unanimous Buddhist and Jain tradition of the contemporaneity of Buddha and Mahāvīra, for the traditional date of the passing away of Mahāvīra is 470 years before the birth of Vikrama which took place 18 years before the foundation of the Vikrama era of 57 BC. The traditional date of the death of Mahāvīra is thus 4705̄71̄8545 BC.[10] The date of the birth of Buddha according to the Cantonese reckoning is 566 BC and this would mean that Buddha was only 21 year old when Mahāvīra died, whereas according to Buddhist canonical texts the former was a renowned religious teacher of long standing when the latter died. The Sri Lankan date of 544 BC for the *nirvāṇa* of Buddha is therefore preferable to the Cantonese date. Since Ajātaśatru ascended the throne eight years before this date, the date of his accession was 552 BC. This one date allows us to fix the dates of all the kings of the four pre-Mauryan dynasties whose account is given in the Purāṇas. We begin with the Kṣemadharmajas whose chronology may be tabulated as follows:

Kṣemadharman	630 — 604 BC
Kṣatraujas	604 — 580 BC
Bimbisāra	580 — 552 BC
Ajātaśatru	552 — 527 BC
Darśaka	527 — 503 BC
Udāyin	503 — 470 BC
Nandivardhana	470 — 446 BC
Mahānandin	446 — 422 BC

Since the dynasty of the Pradyotas came to an end at the same time as that of the Kṣemadharmajas, their chronology would be as follows:

Pradyota	560 — 537 BC
Pālaka	537 — 513 BC
Āryaka	513 — 492 BC
Viśākhayūpa	492 — 442 BC
Avantivardhana	442 — 422 BC

It is worth observing that the date of Pradyota agrees with the fact that he was a younger contemporary of Bimbisāra and continued to rule during the greater part of the reign of Ajātaśatru.

The Śiśunāgas to whom a total period of 65 years is assigned by the Purāṇas must have ruled from 422 to 357 BC, while the Nandas who came to power in 357 BC and ruled for 40 years must have been exterminated by Candragupta Maurya in 317 BC. The date of the accession of Candragupta according to the Purāṇic chronology is thus 317 BC which is wonderfully accurate. The date usually assigned to the foundation of Mauryan empire by Candragupta is 321 BC, but since Eudemos continued to stay in the Panjāb till 317 BC and since Candragupta is believed to have conquered the Magadhan empire of the Nandas after subjugating the bordering Panjāb region[11] he must not have ascended the throne before 317 BC. The Purāṇic chronology of pre-Mauryan kings is thus in complete accord with the traditional date of the *nirvāṇa* of Buddha as well as with the true date of the accession of Candragupta Maurya.

The Haryaṅka dynasty was preceded by the Bṛhadratha dynasty in the region of Magadha. This dynasty consisted of 32 kings of whom the Purāṇas regard 16 as past kings and the remaining as the future kings. The penultimate verse of the account of Bṛhadratha kings, occurring in one of the manuscripts of the *Matsya Purāṇa*, which Pargiter calls 'j' *Matsya*, gives a very invaluable information in the following words: "These sixteen kings are to be known as the future Bṛhadrathas; their kingdom will last 723 years". It is clear that by 'their kingdom', the author of the verse meant the kingdom of the Bṛhadrathas. But some later editor misunderstood it as applying only to the future kings and so added another verse in which he gave the figure 1000 years, for the total duration of the kingdom. This created the untenable position that whereas the future 16 kings reigned for 723 years, the past 16 kings reigned only for 277 years. So the later editors of the Purāṇas omitted this verse altogether from the Purāṇas though it somehow lingered unnoticed in the *j Matsya* manuscript. We have, therefore, no reason to doubt that the figure of 723 years stood for the total duration of the Bṛhadratha dynasty. The duration of 723 years for 32 kings seems worthy of credence also, firstly because it is within the range of possibility, for the average reign period would be about 22½ years, and secondly because such an odd number could hardly have been concocted. Since this dynasty was destroyed by the founder of the Haryaṅka dynasty in 630 BC, it must have been founded in 630+723=1353 BC.

According to the evidence of the Purāṇas, ten kings of the Bṛhadratha dynasty ruled before the Bhārata war. For this comparatively short period of 10 generations we may, not unreasonably, assign an average of 25 years for each generation. The total duration of the reigns of these ten kings would thus be 250 years. The date of the Bhārata war would then be 1353-250=1103 or in round numbers 1100 BC.

The marine archaeological excavations in the Arabian sea near the town of Dvārakā in Gujarat led by Dr. S. R. Rao have proved the truth of the *Mahābhārata* story according to which the ancient city of Dvārakā was washed away by the sea soon after the Bhārata war. The trapezoid three-holed anchors that were discovered there are almost identical with the anchors found in the bronze age sites of Ugarit in Syria which belong to a period ranging from the fourteenth to twelfth century BC. Thus according to archaeological evidence Dvārakā was founded sometime in the twelfth century BC at the latest. The date of the Bhārata war which we have arrived at on the basis of Purāṇic evidence is fully in consonance with this date of Dvārakā, for if we place the Bhārata war in 1100 BC, the antiquity of Dvārakā, which was founded only a few decades before this war, is automatically carried back to the twelfth century BC.

Thus the true date of the Bhārata war, and so of the coronation of Yudhiṣṭhira which immediately followed it, could not have been much earlier than 1100 BC. The year 3102 BC must have originally been the date of some other event, probably of the arrival of Aryans in India, and was wrongly regarded as the date of the coronation of Yudhiṣṭhira.

References

1. It is sometime argued by the supporters of the traditional date of 3102 BC that there could have been loss or omission of some names in the list of kings that ruled between the Bhārata war and the foundation of the Haryaṅka dynasty of Magadha, resulting in such a high average of the reign periods of the kings. This possibility is, however, ruled out by the fact that the Purāṇas

assign a definite number to kings of the Bṛhadratha dynasty of Magadha, which was founded sometime before the Bhārata war and from which the Hariyaṅka dynasty wrested the kingdom of Magadha.

The relevant hemistich is as follows:

"द्वा त्रिंशच्च नृपा ह्येते भवितारो बृहद्रथात् ।

dvā triṁśacca nṛpā hyete, bhavitāro bṛhadrathāt

That is, there will be 32 kings in this dynasty beginning with Bṛhadrath. (Vāyu p. 99, 309, *Matsya* 271, 29)

Of these 32 kings, ten are said to have ruled before the Bhārata war so that the kings of this dyansty who ruled after the Bhārata war were twenty-two in number. They were followed by eight generations of kings in the Hariyaṅka dynasty, two in the Śiśunāga dynasty and two in the Nanda dynasty before the foundation of the Maurya empire by Candragupta. Thus the number of generations of kings that ruled in Magadha after the Bhārata war and before the accession of Candragupta Maurya was exactly thirty-four.

2. Many scholars identify this Parikṣit with Parikṣit II who succeeded Yudhiṣṭhira. Since the coronation of Mahāpadma Nanda took place in 357 BC, as will be shown later in this chapter, the date of birth of Parikṣit II according to this identification would be 357+1050=1407 BC. As according to the Purāṇas 32 generations of kings ruled in Magadha between the dates of the birth of Parikṣit II and the coronation of Mahāpadma Nanda, the average of each reign would be about 33 years which, for such a long period, is too high to be possible. Even if we take the reading 1015 in place of 1050 as found in some of the Purāṇas, it does not make any material difference.

3. The correct forms are *viṁśati* and *caturviṁśati*.

4. *Cambridge History of India,* Vol. I, p. 310.

5. Rājagṛha was an extension of the ancient capital Girivraja and was so called because it grew around the new palace built by king Bimbisāra.

6. Thinking that Mahāpadma Nanda must have immediately succeeded his father Mahānandin, some early Purāṇic copyist seems to have removed the two intervening Śiśunāga kings from

their proper place in the genealogical lists.

7. The difference of one year between the actual aggregate of the two reigns and the total assigned to the dynasty can easily be accounted for by the probability that the reign period of Śiśunāga was actually 39 years and some months and was rounded off as 40 years. The true total of both reigns was thus only 65 years and not 66 years.
8. The use of the word Śiśunāgas in plural here was no doubt originally meant to include the brief reign of the young children of Kākavarṇa under the guardianship of Nanda.
9. Relying on the figure 88 some late editor assigned a total of 100 years to the Nandas which is clearly wrong. The length of the period from the birth of Mahāpadma to the extinction of his family was no doubt 105 years.
10. The Jain author Hemacandra who lived in the twelfth century AD gives the date 467 BC for the demise of Mahāvīra, but as this date goes against the clear statement of the Buddhist *Dīgha Nikāya* and *Majjhima Nikāya* according to which Mahāvīra died before Buddha, it cannot be accepted.
11. A curious story found in the Jain *Pariśiṣṭaparvan* and the Buddhist *Mahāvaṁsaṭīkā* relates that while wandering Candragupta heard an old woman saying that the cause of his failure was that he revolted against Magadha before conquering the border regions and that realising his mistake he conquered the border regions before invading the Magadhan empire.

9

Was Vyāsa the Author of the Traditional Eighteen Purāṇas?

THE Purāṇas are a very important branch of Sanskrit literature. Their traditionally recognized number is eighteen and they are all attributed to the great *ṛṣi* Vyāsa Pārāśarya who was a contemporary of the heroes of the *Mahābhārata* war. Born in the family of the Vedic *ṛṣi* Vasiṣṭha, Vyāsa was a great sage whose name occurs in the Vedic works known as the *Sāmavidhāna Brāhmaṇa* and the *Taittirīya Āraṇyaka*. This attribution of the Purāṇas to Vyāsa has been the cause of the blind reverence in which these works are held by the common Hindu, who, even when he is aware of the glaring contradictions between one Purāṇa and another, seeks to reconcile them because of his faith in their common authorship. What is, however, a matter of bewilderment is the fact that some of the Purāṇas contain strange myths about many of the great characters of ancient India which are totally absent in the other Purāṇas which also deal exhaustively with those characters. This no doubt goes to show that all the Purāṇas could not have been composed by the same person. Some positive proof, however, is needed to produce firm conviction in the minds of those who are accustomed to the belief that Vyāsa was the author of all the eighteen Purāṇas.

Luckily some of the Purāṇas themselves unambiguously declare that Vyāsa composed only one *Purāṇa Saṁhitā*, and that the number of Purāṇas began to grow shortly after his passing away. Three of the most important Purāṇas, *Brahmāṇḍa*, *Vāyu* and *Viṣṇu*, clearly say: "Vyāsa, the master of Purāṇic subject, composed a Purāṇa Saṁhitā with tales, anecdotes, songs and lores that had come down from ages."[1]

Vyāsa has been called here the master of Purāṇic subject-matter which has been explained as consisting of tales, anecdotes, songs and lores coming down from ages. It may naturally be asked as to what these tales, anecdotes, songs and lores were about, how they originated, and who were responsible for preserving and handing them down from generation to generation before they were collected and edited by Vyāsa.

The Purāṇas luckily throw light on these questions also. The *Vāyu* and *Padma Purāṇa*s clearly say that it was the special duty of *sūta*s or bards to preserve the genealogies of godly *ṛṣi*s, illustrious kings and famous heroes.[2] That the institution of *sūta*s was very ancient is proved by their mention in the Vedic literature. The *sūta* is mentioned in the *Yajurveda Saṁhitā*s and *Atharvaveda*.[3] In the latter he is called *rājakṛt*, i.e., king-maker which no doubt means that his duty was to perpetuate the name of his patron by keeping a record of his lineage and achievements. In the *Saṁhitā*s of the Black *Yajurveda* and in two of the *Brāhmaṇas*[4] he is one of the eleven *ratnin*s or members of the royal entourage. In post-Vedic period the *sūta* was both a charioteer and a bard, but this does not seem to have been the case in the Vedic times.

The question naturally arises as to who these *sūta*s were. According to the *Smṛti*s the son of a kṣatriya from a *brāhmaṇa* woman was called a *sūta*. The Vedic *sūta*s, however, could not have been a mixed caste because in the Vedic period brāhmaṇas, kṣatriyas and vaiśyas were classes rather than castes and marriage between them did not result in the birth of persons of mixed castes. Fortunately Kauṭilya dispels all doubts on the subject. According to him the *sūta* mentioned in the Purāṇas was different from the later *sūta* and distinct from both brāhmaṇas and kṣatriyas.[5] That he was not a brāhmaṇa is proved by the Purāṇas themselves which say that the *sūta* had no claim at all to the exposition of the Vedas.[6] It is equally certain that he did not belong to the royal class. It is thus clear that like persons of various other professions he was a viś or commoner.

The material handed down by the *sūta*s from very early times came to be called *purāṇa*, a name which appears to be the abridged form of some such word as *purāṇam ākhyānam*, i.e., old narrative.[7] That this narrative existed even in the early Vedic period is proved by the mention of *purāṇa* with the *ṛk*s, the *sāman*s and the *yajus* in the *Atharvaveda*.[8] It was this floating narrative which was transmitted in the form of tales, anecdotes and songs and which was edited and given a definite shape by Vyāsa in his *Purāṇa Saṁhitā*. There is also a tradition preserved in the Purāṇas which informs us that the original Purāṇa dealt with five topics, viz., creation, dissolution, the ages of the progenitors of mankind, genealogies, and accounts of persons mentioned in the genealogies.[9] It thus appears that Vyāsa incorporated in his *Purāṇa Saṁhitā* not only the genealogies and stories of kings and *ṛṣis* handed down by the *sūta*s but also the ancient lore about the origin, duration and dissolution of the world.

This *Purāṇa Saṁhitā* was given the final form five generations later in the reign of the Bhārata king Adhisīmakṛṣṇa by the *sūta* Lomaharṣaṇa who has been mistakenly called a disciple of Vyāsa. Thus the original *Purāṇa Saṁhitā* was completed about 1000 BC if we regard the Bhārata war to have taken place about 1100 BC. This history of the kings who followed Adhisīmakṛṣṇa continued to be added, but it was written in the form of a prophecy to mark off the time of the original compilation. Some Purāṇas further inform us that three of the pupils of Lomaharṣaṇa composed three independent *Purāṇa Saṁhitā*s on the basis of the original *Purāṇa Saṁhitā*.[10] Thus the gradual multiplication of the Purāṇas is admitted by the ancient Purāṇas themselves which do not bear out the later belief that all the

Purāṇas were composed by Vyāsa.

That there was originally only one *Purāṇa Saṁhitā* need not be doubted. The contention of Winternitz that there never was originally one Purāṇa any more than there was one original *Brāhmaṇa* whence all the *Brāhmaṇa*s sprang or one original Upaniṣad whence all the Upaniṣads sprang[11] is a counsel of dispair. The learned scholar forgot that no ancient Indian work has ever claimed that all the *Brāhmaṇa*s sprang from one *Brāhmaṇa* or that all the Upaniṣads sprang from one Upaniṣad whereas the Purāṇas clearly and indubitably assert that there was originally only one *Purāṇa Saṁhitā*. Moreover, some elements in the contents of most of the Purāṇas are practically identical, pointing to a common source, while this is not the case with the *Brāhmaṇa*s and the Upaniṣads.

It now remains to be seen how the original Purāṇa was transformed into the present Purāṇas. It has been seen that already a few decades after the compilation of the original *Purāṇa Saṁhitā* three independent *Purāṇa Saṁhitā*s sprang up. It is recorded in one of the Purāṇas that the *sūta* Lomaharṣaṇa got this name because his recitation of the Purāṇa before the *ṛṣi*s performing the twelve-year sacrifice in the Naimiṣa forest[12] thrilled the audience and made their hair erect.[13] This must not have been the only occasion on which it was narrated. It must have been usual to recite it in public assemblies and the people must have heard the deeds of their national heroes with delight. As time passed this recitation must have become more and more popular and must have attracted ever-increasing number of listeners. This popularity was naturally exploited by the priests of different sects who began gradually to appropriate the Purāṇas for expounding the religious doctrines of their own sects. These persons were, moreover, not, as Witnernitz rightly says, the learned brāhmaṇas, the Veda knowers, but the rather uneducated temple priests who used them for the glorification of the deities whom they served and in later times more and more for the recommendation of the temples and places of pilgrimages in which they maintained and often enriched themselves.[14] The contents as well as the number of Purāṇas thus continued to multiply till it was recognized that the Purāṇas are eighteen in number.

The internal evidence of the Purāṇas makes it absolutely clear that they were written at widely different times. As a rule, the later the Purāṇa the more its historical matter is burdened with explanatory or laudatory myths and the latest Purāṇas are altogether relieved of historical matter. Reversely, the older the Purāṇa the less its genealogies are burdened with myths and the more they approximate to the Vedic evidence. Judged from this the oldest Purāṇas so far as genealogies and accounts of persons mentioned in the genealogies are concerned are the *Brahma*, the *Vāyu*, the *Brahmāṇḍa* and the *Matsya* all of which purport to be narrated by the *sūta* Lomaharṣaṇa. Later than these are the *Kūrma*, the *Liṅga*, the *Garuḍa* and the *Viṣṇu Purāṇas* and still later are the *Agni*, the *Bhāgavata* and the *Padma Purāṇas*. Among the remaining Purāṇas the *Mārkaṇḍeya* contains very little genealogical matter, the *Bhaviṣya* professedly does not deal with the ancient past and the other five viz., the *Nārada*, the *Brahmavaivarta*, the *Varāha*, the *Vāmana* and the *Skanda* are purely sectarian works free from all historical matter.

The chronology of the Purāṇas is, however, not as easy as this. For instance the *Brahma*, the *Brahmāṇḍa* and the *Matsya* whose genealogical account is ancient contain other material which is comparatively quite late. Reversely, some of the very late Purāṇas like the *Padma* contain some ancient material also. The *Mārkaṇḍeya* whose genealogical material is not of much value appears to be quite ancient if we judge it from the other material that it contains. It is the least sectarian of the Purāṇas which tended to become more and more sectarian with the passage of time. If we cast a glance over the entire contents of the Purāṇas the oldest Purāṇas appear to be the *Vāyu*, the

Brahmāṇḍa and *Matsya* all of which, barring the interpolated portion, must have been composed by the beginning of the fourth century AD. The *Mārkaṇḍeya*, the *Brahma*, the *Kūrma*, the *Liṅga*, the *Garuḍa* and the *Viṣṇu* come next followed by the *Agni*, the *Bhāgavata* and the *Padma*. The latest Purāṇas are no doubt the *Nārada*, the *Brahmavaivarta*, the *Varāha*, the *Vāmana*, the *Skanda* and the *Bhaviṣya* in its present form. All the eighteen Purāṇas seem to have been composed by 1000 AD, since they are all mentioned by Alberuni.

What applies to the Purāṇas also applies to the *Mahābhārata* which too is popularly believed to be a creation of Vyāsa. The internal evidence of the great epic indicates that it was originally called Jaya[15], since it narrated only the events leading to the victory of the Pāṇḍavas over the Kauravas. This original poem probably consisted of only 8800 verses.[16] These verses, however, appeared so intricate after the lapse of some centuries[17] that the need for amplification was felt. The poem thus swelled to the size of 24,000 verses and came to be called Bhārata. There were, however, still no episodes in it.[18] Its popularity eventually led to its conversion into a compendium of knowledge with the addition of all kinds of episodes and didactic matter raising its bulk to 1,00,000 verses. In its final form it received the name *Mahābhārata*. There can be no doubt that the later additions of *Mahābhārata* belong to the same period as the later Purāṇas.

The great sage Vyāsa was thus not responsible for the numerous absurd unedifying and sectarian myths, legends and doctrines that found their way into the present Purāṇas and the *Mahābhārata* during the decadent period of Indian history. He was the author of only one *Purāṇa Saṁhitā*, and of one epic poem of moderate size called Jaya.

References

1. आख्यानैश्चाप्युपाख्यानैर्गाथाभिः कल्पजोक्तिभिः ।
पुराणसंहितां चक्रे पुराणार्थविशारदः ।।

Brahmāṇḍa II, 34, 21; *Vāyu* 60, 21; *Viṣṇu* III, 6, 16.

2. *Vāyu* 1, 31-2; *Padma* V, 1, 27-8.
3. *Kāṭhaka* XV, 4; *Maitrāyanī* II, 65; *Taittirīya* I, 8, 91; *Atharvaveda* III, 5, 7.
4. *Taittirīya* I, 7, 3, 1; *Śatapatha* V, 3, 1, 5.
5. *Arthaśāstra* III, 7.
6. *Vāyu* I,33. *Bhāgavata* I, 4, 13 regards the *sūta* conversant with the whole realm of literature with the exception of the Veda. According to a late myth occurring in the *Bhāgavata* (X, 78,20-32) the *sūta* Lomaharṣaṇa, though not a brāhmaṇa, was given the seat of a brāhmaṇa by the sages assembled at Naimiṣa and hence when Balarāma killed him he incurred the sin of killing a brāhmaṇa. The three most ancient Purāṇas, *Vāyu*, *Brahmāṇḍa* and *Matsya*, however, clearly say that Lomaharṣaṇa was a contemporary of Adhisīmakṛṣṇa, sixth in descent from Arjuna, the hero of the Bhārata war. Balarāma, on the other hand, was a contemporary of Arjuna and died soon after the Bhārata war. How then could he have killed Lomaharṣaṇa?
7. Winternitz, *History of Indian Literature,* Vol. I, p. 518.
8. XI, 7, 24.
9. सर्गश्च प्रतिसर्गश्च वंशो मन्वन्तराणि च ।
   वंश्यानुचरितं चेति पुराणं पंचलक्षणम् ।।

   Vāyu 4, 10-1; *Brahmāṇḍa* I, 1, 37-8; *Matsya* 53,65; *Viṣṇu* III, 6, 25.
10. *Vāyu* 61, 55-62; *Brahmāṇḍa* II, 35, 63-70; *Viṣṇu* III, 6, 17-19; *Agni* 279, 10-13.
11. *History of Indian Literature,* Vol. I, p. 522.
12. This Naimiṣa forest was on the bank of the river Dṛṣadvatī near Kurukṣetra and was different from the modern Nimsar near Sitapur in Uttar Pradesh.
13. *Vāyu* I, 16.
14. *History of Indian Literature,* Vol. I, pp. 528-29.
15. The first verse of the present *Mahābhārata* exhorts the reader to recite the 'Jaya' after obeisance to Nārāyaṇa and others.
16. *Mahābhārata* I, 1, 81.
17. *Ibid* I, 1, 82.
18. *Ibid* I, 7, 102-3.

10

Was Vālmīki a Robber in his Youth?

THE *Rāmāyaṇa*, often designated as the *ādikāvya*[1], is not only the first but also the most popular epic of the Sanskrit language and its author Vālmīki, therefore, occupies a high place among the poets of the world. It is, however, a pity that this great poet has been the victim of late myths which were invented in contravention of all ancient evidence only to prove how a base metal could be converted into pure gold by devotion to Śiva or Rāma. These myths are found in a late passeage of the *Mahābhārata*, the late *Skanda Purāṇa* and a very late Rāma poem called the *Adhyātma Rāmāyaṇa*. The myths found in these works reappear in certain mediaeval works composed in Sanskrit and other Indian languages. A detailed account of these myths is being given below.

Chapters 17 and 18 of book XIII of the *Mahābhārata* have evidently been written by some devout Śaiva with the object of popularizing Śiva worship. Chapter 17 recounts one thousand names of Śiva and the following chapter relates a number of myths not found elsewhere, the heroes of which are the most celebrated of ancient sages like Kapila, Vālmīki, Paraśurāma, Viśvāmitra and Gṛtsamada who are said to have been freed from sin by repeating these thousand names. For making them free from sin it was necesary to ascribe some sins to them. Hence Paraśurāma is said to have killed his father and a number of brāhmaṇas and Vālmīki is similarly accused of slaying brāhmaṇas. The spurious nature of this chapter is clear from the fact that nowhere else is Paraśurāma said to have killed his father or the brāhmaṇas. What is true of Paraśurāma is also true of Vālmīki who has never been called a brāhmaṇa-slayer in any of the ancient works including the ancient portions of the *Mahābhārata*. Moreover, Gṛtsamada, Viśvāmitra and Paraśurāma were Vedic seers who were devoted to the Vedic gods like Agni, Indra and Varuṇa and not to Śiva, and even Vālmīki, though belonging to the post-Vedic period, was not far differnt in religious beliefs, for in the genuine *Rāmāyaṇa* the highest gods are still Indra and Varuṇa rather than Śiva and Viṣṇu. These two chapters of book XIII of the *Mahābhārata* are thus not only late but also full of absurdities.

The *Skanda Purāṇa* is one of the latest works in Purāṇa literature. In fact it hardly deserves to be called a Purāṇa for there is little in it that corresponds to the five characteristics of a Purāṇa. Four sections of this voluminous work named *Vaiṣṇava khaṇḍa*, *Avantī khaṇḍa*, *Nāgara khaṇḍa* and *Prabhāsa khaṇḍa* contain myths about Vālmīki. According to one myth he was a hunter in his former life who in consequence of repeating the name of Rāma was born in a brāhmaṇa family as Vālmīki and composed the *Rāmāyaṇa*. The other three myths portray him as a brāhmaṇa who earned his living by killing and robbing wayfarers and became Vālmīki when he emerged from an anthill (*valmīka*) by which he was covered in consequence of being absorbed in repeating certain *mantra*s taught to him by the seven sages whom he originally wanted to kill but later spared.

The myths appearing in the *Skanda Purāṇa* were utilized by the author of the late *Adhyātma Rāmāyaṇa* in coining his own myth about Vālmīki. In the sixth Canto of the *Ayodhyā kāṇḍa* of this *Rāmāyaṇa* Vālmīki himself has been made to say that in his childhood he was brought up among the rude Kirātas and was a brāhmaṇa only in name, that on growing up he fell in the company of robbers and began to rob and kill wayfarers, that he was at an accidental meeting exhorted by the seven sages to repeat for an indefinite time the reverse form of Rāma (i.e., *marā*), that while absorbed in repeating this word he was covered with an anthill and that he was ultimately taken out of that anthill by those very seven sages and proclaimed to be a sage named Vālmīki.

It is necessary to examine these myths before marshalling the ancient evidence about the genesis of Vālmīki. It is clear that these myth-makers had only two objects in view while fabricating these myths. The common object of all the myths occurring in the *Skanda Purāṇa* and the *Adhyātma Rāmāyaṇa* was to explain the name Vālmīki. Stories invented to explain the names of ancient heroes and heroines are legion in the Purāṇas and this tendency of Purāṇic interpolaters was rightly decried by Pargiter long ago on pp. 75-76 of his *Ancient Indian Historical Tradition* in the following words: "Most of such stories have been coined out of the names themselves, sometimes fanciful, sometimes mistaken and sometimes absurd. . . . Many if not most are obviously late fabrication, being fashioned with grotesque ingenuity." To this category these myths about Vālmīki found in the *Skanda Purāṇa* and the *Adhyātma Rāmāyaṇa*, whose authors, being ignorant of the true ancestry of the sage, derived his name from *valmīka* (anthill). The other object of at least two of these myths was to show the miraculous effect of repeating the name of Rāma which could transform a robber into a sage.

That these myths run counter to the evidence of the *Rāmāyaṇa* including its interpolated parts is crystal clear. Any reader of the *Rāmāyaṇa* can see that it does not attribute any miraculous power to the name of Rāma. In fact it is evident from the genuine *Rāmāyaṇa* that Vālmīki treated Rāma only as an ideal hero and not as an incarnation of God. It is therefore absurd to say that he was given to muttering the name of Rāma at any time in his life. Secondly even the interpolated portions of the

Rāmāyaṇa, which were no doubt written long before Kālidāsa who could not have flourished later then the fifth century AD, do not give the slightest indication that Vālmīki was a cruel marauder and robber in his youth. On the contrary, a charming story about the early life of Vālmīki, found in the first book of the *Rāmāyaṇa*, depicts him as full of the milk of human kindness who was so deeply moved even by the grief of a female bird when her mate was killed by a Niṣāda that he pronounced a curse on the tribe of the hunter. The myths found in the *Skanda Purāṇa* and the *Adhyātma Rāmāyaṇa* are thus totally discredited by the *Rāmāyaṇa* of Vālmīki.

In contrast to the *Skanda Purāṇa* and the *Adhyātma Rāmāyaṇa* which are silent on the lineage of Vālmīki, all the ancient works which mention the sage call him a descendant of Bhṛgu and Cyavana.[2] Thus verse 26 occurring in Canto 94 of the *Uttarakāṇḍa* of the *Rāmāyaṇa* says: "(This *Rāmāyaṇa* consisting of) twenty-four thousand verses and a hundred episodes was composed by the austere descendant of Bhṛgu".

The *Mahābhārata* (XII,57,40-41) says:

> The (matter of the) following verse was sung formerly with reference to a king by the great-souled descendant of Bhṛgu in the deeds of Rāma narrated by him. 'One should first have a king, then wife and then wealth. How can one have a wife or wealth in the absence of a king'.

The views attributed to Vālmīki in this verse are actually expressed by the poet in his *Rāmāyaṇa* (II, 61, 10) in the following manner:

> In a country having no king one can have neither wealth nor wife. Yet another danger in a country without a king is the loss of truthfulness.

The ancient *Matsya Purāṇa* (12, 51) regards Vālmīki as the

most eminent among the descedants of Bhṛgu in a verse which is as follows:

> Vālmīki, the best among the descendants of Bhṛgu, composed (a poem on) his (i.e., Rāma's) deeds.

The *Padma Purāṇa* (V,8,155) repeats this verse verbatim.

The ancient *Viṣṇu Purāṇa* (III,3,18) gives the personal name Ṛkṣa to Vālmīki and calls him a descendant of Bhṛgu.

Though no definite date can be assigned to the two epics and the three Purāṇas cited above, they are indisputably older than the *Skanda Purāṇa* and the *Adhyātma Rāmāyaṇa* and are therefore more authentic than these two and the other still later works that give different versions of the myth about Vālmīki. Luckily a poet who is assigned to the first century AD by practically all Indologists confirms the evidence of the epics and the *Matsya*, *Padma* and *Viṣṇu Purāṇas* in regarding Vālmīki a descendant of Bhṛgu's grandson Cyavana. This poet is Aśvaghoṣa who in the first Canto of his *Buddhacarita* gives a charming conversation between king Śuddhodana and the brāhmaṇas invited by him for predictions about the future greatness of his new-born son Siddhārtha. When on hearing the predictions the king expresses his scepticism about the future greatness of his son, the brāhmaṇas give a number of examples to prove that descendants often accomplish what the ancestors were incapable of. Some of these examples are as follows:

> Vālmīki first created a metre, whereas (his ancestor) the great *ṛṣi* Cyavana never produced any. The medical science on which Atri never wrote was later expounded by (his descendant) Ātreya. Kuśika never attained Brāhmanhood, but (his descendant Viśvāmitra) son of Gāthin, attained it. Śūra and others were incapable of the famous deeds of (Kṛṣṇa), the descendant of Śūra. Therefore neither age nor descent matters and any one

can attain greatness anywhere in the world, for such marvellous deeds were done by persons of royal and saintly lineage as were never done by their acnestors.[3]

This quotation amply proves that Vālmīki was regarded a descendant of Bhṛgu and Cyavana long before the first century AD.

As a matter of fact the *Pravarādhyāya* of the ancient *Baudhāyana Śrauta Sūtra* which is placed between 800 and 400 BC[4] mentions Vālmīki as a *gotra* in the *Vatsa pakṣa* of the family of Bhṛgu. This name thus could be borne by other persons of this *gotra* and this is proved by the fact that we learn from the *Taittirīya Prātiśākhya* of a phoenecian Vālmīki who was certainly different from the much more famous poet Vālmīki.[5]

This chain of evidence recorded in so many ancient works proves beyond a shadow of doubt that Vālmīki was born in the illustrious family of Bhṛgu and was a tender-hearted and gifted man. It was only after the lapse of long centuries since his birth that he became a victim of myth-makers who wanted to give a fanciful explanation of his name and to show that he was transformed from a villain into a sage by muttering the name of Rāma.

A word may be said about the date of Vālmīki. It is certain that he was not a contemporary of the hero of his epic as the interpolated first and last books of the *Rāmāyaṇa* make him out to be. Rāma certainly belonged to the Vedic age when the language spoken was Vedic Sanskrit whereas Vālmīki composed his epic in classical Sanskrit which could hardly have developed from the former earlier than the eighth century BC. This would, therefore, be the upper limit of Vālmīki's date. As for the lower limit, Jacobi has given convincing reasons to show that the *Rāmāyaṇa* could not have originated later than the sixth century BC. His main arguments are as follows:

1. The only mention of Buddha in the *Rāmāyaṇa* occurs in a passage of the second book. This passage has been proved to be interpolated, so that there is no mention of Buddha in the genuine *Rāmāyaṇa*.
2. The only mention of Yavanas or Greeks in the genuine books (II-VI) of the *Rāmāyaṇa* occurs in a Canto of book IV which has been shown to be an interpolation. Thus the genuine *Rāmāyaṇa* does not mention the Yavanas.
3. No mention is made in the *Rāmāyaṇa* of the city of Pāṭaliputra, founded by king Udāyin in 500 BC, although according to it Rāma passed the very spot where that city stood before he reached Viśālā and finally Mithilā. Had Pāṭaliputra exised at the time of the composition of the *Rāmāyaṇa* it could not have failed to be mentioned.
4. It is further a noteworthy fact that the capital of Kosala is in the *Rāmāyaṇa* regularly called Ayodhyā, while the Buddhists, Jains, Greeks and Patañjali always give it the name of Sāketa. This points to the fact that the *Rāmāyaṇa* was composed when Ayodhyā's new name Sāketa was still unknown.

Vālmīki, therefore, according to Jacobi, composed the *Rāmāyaṇa* somewhere between 800 and 500 BC and Macdonell concurs with this. Winternitz on the other hand assigns Vālmīki to the third century BC.[6] Now it cannot be denied that even when a poet writes about an event that happened long before his time, he cannot remain totally uninfluenced by the things around him. If, therefore, Vālmīki lived in the third century BC, he must have heard about Jainism and Buddhism and about the Yavanas with whom the Maurya kings of that period had close contacts. Yet there is not even the faintest allusion either to the Jains or the Buddhists or the Yavanas in the genuine *Rāmāyaṇa*. Further if Vālmīki lived in the third century BC it is impossible to explain why he does not mention Ayodhyā's new name Sāketa, even when his story centres round that city, and does not mention the most famous city of Pāṭaliputra in the course of Rāma's journey to Mithilā even though mentioning the smaller city of Viśālā. Lastly it should also be remembered that Vālmīki depicts the whole region lying between the Yamunā in the north and the Indian ocean in the south as covered by forests, whereas in the third century BC, during the age of the Mauryas, the Cola, Pāṇḍya, Kerala and Satiyaputra states are known to have flourished in the far south. If Vālmīki had been living in the third century BC he could not have failed to mention these states. It is a pity that Winternitz did not take these facts into consideration in determining the date of Vālmīki. We cannot therefore help coming to the conclusion at which Jacobi arrived long ago that Vālmīki flourished somewhere between 800 and 500 BC, probably in the seventh century BC.

References

1. Though the original work Jaya out of which the present *Mahābhārata* grew was composed earlier than the *Rāmāyaṇa*, it is not regarded as the *ādikāvya* of the Sanskrit language for three reasons: (1) It was really an *itihāsa* and not a *kāvya* proper, (2) Its language was probably closer to the Vedic than to the classical Sanskrit, (3) It no longer exists and even the ancient portions of the present *Mahābhārata* are later than the original part of the *Rāmāyaṇa*.
2. Bulcke in his '*Rāmakathā* ' (pp. 35-45) seems to attach greater value to the *Skanda Purāṇa*, the *Adhyātma Rāmāyaṇa* and even such mediaeval works as the *Bhaktamāla* and the *Rāmacaritamānasa* and calls the works in which Vālmīki has been called a descendant of Bhṛgu as late, though they are all indisputably more ancient than the *Skanda Purāṇa* and the *Adhyātma Rāmāyaṇa*. The fact that members of certain castes are trying to establish their relationship with such great men of the past as Kṛṣṇa, Vālmīki and Aśoka in order to rise in social scale is absolutely of no consequence in determining the origin of these celebrities. Sanskrit being the close preserve of the Āryan elite in ancient times, it is indeed impossible to believe, in

contravention of ancient evidence, that the first poem of this language was composed by a non-Āryan tribesman.

3. वाल्मीकिरादौ च ससर्ज पद्यं जग्रन्थ यन्न च्यवनो महर्षिः ।
चिकित्सितं यच्च चकार नात्रिः पश्चात्तदात्रेय ऋषिर्जगाद ।।

यच्च द्विजत्वं कुशिको न लेभे तद्गाथिनः सूनुरवाप राजन् ।
ख्यातानि कर्माणि च यानि शौरेः शूरादयस्तेष्वबला बभूवुः ।।

तस्मात्प्रमाणं न वयो न वंशः कश्चित्क्वचिच्छ्रैष्ठ्यमुपैति लोके ।
राज्ञामृषीणां च हि तानि तानि कृतानि पुत्रैरकृतानि पूर्वैः ।। 43-46

Some manuscripts have the reading वाल्मीकिनादः in place of वाल्मीकिरादौ.The translation in that case would be "the voice of Vālmīki" in place of "Valmīki first". It is a pity that D.C. Sircar in his *Problems of the Rāmāyaṇa* (p. 5) puts in the mouth of Aśvaghoṣa what he never said. The poet nowhere says that Cyavana made an "attempt to write the *Rāmakathā*" but it was "either defective or remained incomplete". He is talking only about the composition of "*padya*" in which Vālmīki excelled his ancestor Cyavana. If somebody says that Bāṇa composed a *gadyakāvya* which his ancestor Vālmīki could not, would it mean that Vālmīki also attempted to write 'Harṣacarita'? In fact Aśvaghoṣa could never have attributed a *Rāmakathā* to Cyavana because he must have known that Cyavana lived long before Rāma. According to the unanimous testimony of the Purāṇas, which is supported by the *Śatapatha Brāhmaṇa*, Cyavana was the son-in-law of Manu's son Śaryāti, brother of Ikṣvāku. There is a gap of about 70 generations between Rāma and his ancestor Ikṣvāku which means, that Ikṣvāku's brother Śaryāti and therefore the latter's son-in-law Cyavana lived more than a millennium before Rāma. How could he then attempt to write *Rāmakathā*? It may further be added that Cyavana is mentioned as an ancient sage in several hymns addressed to Aśvins occurring in the oldest portions of the *Ṛgveda*. That he is the same Cyavana as mentioned in the *Śatapatha Brāhmaṇa* and the Purāṇas is proved by the fact that the Ṛgvedic hymns agree with these works in holding that the sage was freed from old age by the Aśvins. Rāma on the other hand is not mentioned at all at least in the older nine books of the *Ṛgveda* although the names of several of his ancestors such as Ikṣvāku, Māndhātṛ, Purukutsa, Trasadasyu and Trayaruṇa occur in these books.The *Ṛgveda* also thus makes it clear that Cyavana lived far earlier than Rāma and so could not have composed a *Rāmakathā*. The other issues raised by Dr. Sirvar have been fully discussed by me in my article entitled "A Fresh Appraisal of the Historicity of Indian Epics" published in *Annals of the Bhandarkar Oriental Research Institue,* Vol. LXIII, 1982.

4. *History and Culture of the Indian People,* Vol. I, *The Vedic Age*, p. 447.

5. Both Weber and Jacobi hold this view. Bulcke's contention (*Rāmakathā*, p. 33) that the *Mahābhārata* mentions two other Vālmīkis besides the great poet is baseless. The *ṛṣi* Vālmīki mentioned in various *parvas* of the *Mahābhārata* is undoubtedly none other than the famous poet Vālmīki. *Mahābhārata* V, 101 describes the various species of the semi-mythical birds called *garuḍas* or *suparṇas* (eagles). They are called cruel snake-eaters and are by virtue of their aggressive deeds (*karmaṇā*) likened to kṣatriyas. The fact that one of their species bears the same name as the sage Vālmīki does not make them human beings any more than the skylarks who bear the same name as the sage Bharadvāja.

6. The arguments of Winternitz have been examined by me in my book *India in the Vedic Age,* 2nd edn., pp. 31-36.

Appendix

THE genuine portion of the *Bālakāṇḍa* of Vālmīki's *Rāmāyaṇa* originally forming the commencement of its *Ayodhyākāṇḍa*.

Canto I (Canto V of the present *Rāmāyaṇa*)

कोसलो नाम मुदितः स्फीतो जनपदो महान् ।
निविष्टः सरयूतीरे प्रभूतधनधान्यवान् ।। 1।।

अयोध्या नाम नगरी तत्रासील्लोकविश्रुता ।
मनुना मानवेन्द्रेण या पुरी निर्मिता स्वयम् ।। 2 ।।

आयता दश च द्वे च योजनानि महापुरी ।
श्रीमती त्रीणि विस्तीर्णा सुविभक्तमहापथा ।। 3 ।।

राजमार्गेण महता सुविभक्तेन शोभिता ।
मुक्तपुष्पविकीर्णेन जलसिक्तेन नित्यशः ।। 4 ।।

तां तु राजा दशरथो महाराष्ट्रविवर्धनः ।
पुरीमावासयामास दिवि देवपतिर्यथा ।। 5 ।।

कपाटतोरणवतीं सुविभक्तान्तरापणाम् ।
सर्वयन्त्रायुधवतीमुपेतां सर्वशिल्पिभिः ।। 6 ।।

सूतमागधसंबाधां श्रीमतीमतुलप्रभाम् ।
उच्चाट्टालध्वजवतीं शतघ्नीशतसंकुलाम् ।। 7 ।।

वधूनाटकसंघैश्च संयुक्तां सर्वतः पुरीम् ।
उद्यानाभ्रवणोपेतां महतीं सालमेखलाम् ।। 8 ।।

दुर्गगम्भीरपरिधां दुर्गामन्यैर्दुरासदाम् ।
वाजिवारणसंपूर्णां गोभिरुष्ट्रैःखरैस्तथा ।। 9 ।।

सामन्तराजसंघैश्च बलिकर्मभिरावृताम् ।

नानादेशनिवासैश्च वणिग्भिरूपशोभिताम् ।। 10 ।।

प्रासादै रत्नविकृतैः पर्वतैरिवशोभिताम्।
कूटागारैश्च संपूर्णामिन्द्रस्येवामरावतीम् ।। 11 ।।

चित्रामष्टापदाकारां वरनारीगणैर्युताम् ।
सर्वरत्नसमाकीर्णां विमानगृहशोभिताम् ।। 12 ।।

गृहगाढामविच्छिद्रां सममूमौ निवेशिताम् ।
शालितण्डुल संपूर्णामिक्षुकाण्डरसोदकाम् ।। 13 ।।

दुन्दुभीभिर्मृदंगैश्च वीणाभिः पणवैस्तथा ।
नादितां भृशमत्यर्थं पृथिव्यां तामनुत्तमाम् ।। 14 ।।

विमानमिव सिद्धानां तपसाधिगतं दिवि ।
सुनिवेशितवेश्मान्तां नरोत्तमसमावृताम् ।। 15 ।।

ये च बाणैर्न विध्यन्ति विविक्तमपरापरम् ।
शब्दवेधं च विततं लघुहस्ता विशारदाः ।। 16 ।।

सिंहव्याघ्रवराहाणां मत्तानां नदतां वने ।
हन्तारो निशितैः शस्त्रैर्बलाद्बाहुवलैरपि ।। 17 ।।

तादृशानां सहस्त्रैस्तामभिपूर्णां महारथैः ।
पुरीमावासयामास राजा दशरथस्तदा ।। 18 ।।

तामग्निमद्भिर्गुणवद्भिरावृतां द्विजोत्तमैर्वेदषडंगपारगैः ।
सहस्त्रदैःसत्यरतैर्महात्मभिर् महर्षिकल्पैर्ऋषिमिश्च केवलैः ।। 19 ।।

Canto II (Canto VI of the present *Rāmāyaṇa*)

पुर्यां तस्यामयोध्यायां वेदवित्सर्वसंग्रहः ।
दीर्घदर्शी महातेजाः पौरजानपदप्रियः ।। 1 ।।

इक्ष्वाकूणामतिरथो यज्वा धर्मरतो वशी ।
महर्षिकल्पो राजर्षिस्त्रिषु लोकेषु विश्रुतः ।। 2 ।।

बलवान्निहतामित्रो मित्रवान्विजितेन्द्रियः ।
धनैश्च संचयैश्चान्यैः शक्रवैश्रवणोपमः ।। 3 ।।

यथा मनुर्महातेजा लोकस्य परिरक्षिता ।
तथा दशरथो राजावसज्जगदपालयत् ।। 4 ।।

तेन सत्याभिसन्धेन त्रिवर्गमनुतिष्ठता ।
पालिता सा पुरी श्रेष्ठा इन्द्रेणेवामरावती ।। 5 ।।

तस्मिन् पुरवरे हृष्टा धर्मात्मानो बहुश्रुताः ।
नरास्तुष्टा घनैः स्वैः स्वैरलुब्धा सत्यवादिनः ।। 6 ।।

नाल्पसन्निचयः कश्चिदासीत्तस्मिन्पुरोत्तमे ।
कुटुम्बी यो ह्यसिद्धार्थोऽगवाश्वधनधान्यवान् ।। 7 ।।

कामी वा न कदर्यो वा नृशंसः पुरुषः क्वचित् ।
द्रष्टुं शक्यमयोध्यायां नाविद्वान्न च नास्तिकः ।। 8 ।।

सर्वे नराश्च नार्यश्च धर्मशीलाः सुसंयताः ।
मुदिताः शीलवृत्ताभ्यां महर्षय हवामलाः ।। 9 ।।

नाकुण्डली नामुकुटी नास्त्रग्वी नाल्पभोगवान् ।
नामृष्टो नानुलिप्तांगो नासुगन्धश्च विद्यते ।। 10 ।।

नामृष्टभोजी नादाता नाप्यनंगदनिष्कधृक् ।
नाहस्ताभरणो वापि दृश्यते नाप्यनात्मवान् ।। 11 ।।

नानाहिताग्निर्नायज्वा विप्रो नाप्यसहस्त्रदः ।
कश्चिदासीदयोध्यायां न निर्वृत्तो न संकरः ।। 12 ।।

स्वकर्मनिरता नित्यं ब्राह्मणा विजितेन्द्रियाः ।
दानाध्ययनशीलाश्च संयताश्च प्रतिग्रहे ।। 13 ।।

न नास्तिको नानृतको न कश्चिदबहुश्रुतः ।
नासूयको न चाशक्तो नाविद्वान् विद्यते तदा ।। 14 ।।

न दीनः क्षिप्तचित्तो वा व्यथितो वापि कश्चन ।
कश्चिन्नरो वा नारी वा नाश्रीमान्नाप्यरूपवान् ।
द्रष्टुं शक्यमयोध्यायां नापि राजन्यभक्तिमान् ।। 15 ।।

वर्णेष्वग्र्यचतुर्थेषु देवतातिथिपूजकाः ।
दीर्घायुषो नराः सर्वे धर्मं सत्यं च संश्रिताः ।। 16 ।।

क्षत्रं ब्रह्ममुखं चासीद्विश्याः क्षत्रमनुव्रताः ।
शूद्राः स्वधर्मनिरतास्त्रीन्वर्णानुपचारिणः ।। 17 ।।

सा तेनेक्ष्वाकुनाथेन पुरी सुपरिरक्षिता ।
यथा पुरस्तान्मनुना मानवेन्द्रेण धीमता ।। 18 ।।

योधानामग्निकल्पानां पेशलानाममर्षिणाम् ।
संपूर्णा कृतविद्यानां गुहा केसरिणामिव ।। 19 ।।

काम्बोजविषयेजातै र्बाह्लीकैश्च हयोत्तमैः ।
वनायुजैर्नदीजैश्च पूर्णा हरिहयोपमैः ।। 20 ।।

विन्ध्यपर्वतजैर्मत्तैः पूर्णा हैमवतैरपि ।
मदान्वितैरतिबलैर्मातंगैः पर्वतोपमैः ।। 21 ।।

अञ्जनादपि निष्क्रान्तै र्वामनादपि च द्विपैः ।
भद्रमन्द्रै र्भद्रमृगै मृगमन्द्रैश्च सा पुरी ।। 22 ।।

नित्यमत्तैः सदापूर्णा नागैरचलसंनिभैः ।
सा योजने च द्वे भूयः सत्यनामा प्रकाशते ।। 23 ।।

तां सत्यनामां दृढ़तोरणार्गलां गृहैर्विचित्रैरूपशोभितां शिवाम् ।
पुरीमयोध्यां नृसहस्त्रसंकुलां शाशास वै शक्रसमो महीपतिः ।। 24 ।।

Canto III (Canto VII of the present *Rāmāyaṇa*)

अष्टौ बभूवुर्वीरस्य तस्यामात्या यशस्विनः ।
शुचयश्चानुरक्ताश्च राजकृत्येषु नित्यशः ।। 1 ।।

धृष्टि र्जयन्तो विजयः सिद्धार्थो अर्थसाधकः ।
अशोको मन्त्रपालश्च सुमंत्रश्चाष्टमोऽभवत् ।। 2 ।।

श्रीमन्तश्च महात्मानः शास्त्रज्ञा दृढ़विक्रमाः ।
कीर्तिमन्तः प्रणिहिता यथावचनकारिणः ।। 3 ।।

तेजःक्षमायशःप्राप्ताः स्मितपूर्वाभिभाषिणः ।
क्रोधात्कामार्थ हेतोर्वा न ब्रूयुरनृतं वचः ।। 4 ।।

तेषामविदितं किंचित्स्वेषु नास्ति परेषु वा ।
क्रियमाणं कृतं वापि चारेणापि चिकीर्षितम् ।। 5 ।।

कुशला व्यवहारेषु सौहृदेषु परीक्षिताः ।
प्राप्तकालं यथा दण्डं धारयेयुः सुतेष्वपि ।। 6 ।।

कोशसंग्रहणे युक्ता बलस्य च परिग्रहे ।
अहितं चापि पुरुषं न विहिंस्युरदूषकम् ।। 7 ।।

वीराश्च नियतोत्साहा राजशास्त्रमनुष्ठिताः ।
शुचीनां रक्षितारश्च नित्यं विषयवासिनाम् ।। 8 ।।

ब्रह्मक्षत्रमहिंसन्तस्ते कोशमपूरयन्
सुतीक्ष्णदण्डाः संप्रेक्ष्य पुरुषस्य बलाबलम् ।। 9 ।।

शुचीनामेकबुद्धीनां सर्वेषां संप्रजानताम् ।
नासीत्पुरे वा राष्ट्रे वा मृषावादी नरः क्वचित् ।। 10 ।।

कश्चिन्न दुष्टस्तत्रासीत्परदाररतिर्नरः ।
प्रशान्तं सर्वमेवासीद्राष्ट्रं पुरवरं च तत् ।। 11 ।।

सुवाससः सुवेशाश्च ते च सर्वे सुशीलिनः ।
हितार्थं च नरेन्द्रस्य जाग्रतो नयचक्षुषा ।। 12 ।।

गुरौ गुणगृहीताश्च प्रख्याताश्च पराक्रमैः ।
विदेशेष्वपि विज्ञाताः सर्वतो बुद्धिनिश्चयात् ।। 13 ।।

ईदृशैस्तैरमात्यैस्तु राजा दशरथोऽनघः ।
उपपन्नो गुणौपेतैरन्वशासद्वसुन्धराम् ।। 14 ।।

अवेक्षमाणश्चारेण प्रजा धर्मेण रंजयन् ।
नाध्यगच्छद्विशिष्टं वा तुल्यं वा शत्रुमात्मनः ।। 15 ।।

तैर्मंत्रिभिर्मत्रहितैर्निविष्टैर् वृतोऽनुरक्तैः कुशलैः समर्थैः ।
स पार्थिवो दीप्तिमवाप युक्तस् तेजोमयै र्गोभिरिवोदितोऽर्कः ।। 16 ।।

Canto VI (Canto XI of the present *Rāmāyaṇa*)

ततः काले बहुतिथे कस्मिंश्चित्सुमनोहरे ।
बसन्ते समनुप्राप्ते राज्ञो यष्टुं मनोऽभवत् ।। 1 ।।

ततो राजाऽब्रवीद्वाक्यं सुमंत्रं मंत्रिसत्तमम् ।
सुमंत्रावाहय क्षिप्रमृत्विजो ब्रह्मवादिनः ।। 2 ।।

ततः सुमंत्रस्त्वरितं गत्वा त्वरितविक्रमः ।
समानयत्स तान् विप्रान् समस्तान्वेदपारगान् ।। 3 ।।

सुयज्ञं वामदेवं च जाबालिमथ काश्यपम् ।
पुरोहितं वसिष्ठं च ये चान्ये द्विजसत्तमाः ।। 4 ।।

तान् पूजयित्वा धर्मात्मा राजा दशरथस्तदा ।
इदं धर्मार्थसहितं श्लक्ष्णं वचनमब्रवीत् ।। 5 ।।

मम लालप्यमानस्य पुत्रार्थं नास्ति वै सुखम ।
तदर्थं हयमेधेन यक्ष्यामीति मतिर्मम ।। 6 ।।

तदहं यष्टुमिच्छामि शास्त्रदृष्टेन कर्मणा ।
ऋषिपुत्रप्रभावेन कामान् प्राप्स्यामि चाप्यहम् ।। 7 ।।

ततः साध्विति तद्वाक्यं ब्राह्मणाः प्रत्यपूजयन् ।
वसिष्ठप्रमुखाः सर्वे पार्थिवस्य मुखाध्युतम् ।। 8 ।।

ऋष्यश्रृंगपुरोगाश्च प्रत्यूचुर्नृपतिं तदा ।
संभाराः संभ्रियन्तां ते तुरगश्च विमुच्यताम् ।। 9 ।।

सर्वथा प्राप्स्यसे पुत्रांश्चतुरोऽमितविक्रमान्।
यस्य ते धार्मिकी बुद्धिरियं पुत्रार्थमागता ।। 10 ।।

ततः प्रीतोऽभवद्राजा श्रुत्वा तद्द्विजभाषितम् ।
अमात्यांश्चाब्रवीद्राजा हर्षेणेदं शुभाक्षरम् ।। 11 ।।

गरुणां वचनाच्छीघ्रं संभाराः संभ्रियन्तु मे ।
समर्थाधिष्ठितश्चाश्वः सोपाध्यायो विमुच्यताम् ।। 12 ।।

सरय्वाश्चोत्तरे तीरे यज्ञभूमिर्विधीयताम् ।
शान्तयश्चाभिवर्धन्तां यथाकल्पं यघाविधि ।। 13 ।।

शक्यः कर्तुमयं यज्ञः सर्वेणाषि महीक्षिता ।
नापराधो भवेत्कष्टो यद्यस्मिन् क्रतुसत्तमे ।। 14 ।।

छिद्रंहि मृगयन्तेऽत्र विद्वांसो ब्रह्मराक्षसाः ।
विधिहीनस्य यज्ञस्य सद्यः कर्ता विनश्यति ।। 15 ।।

तद्यथा विधिपूर्वं मे क्रतुरेष समाप्यते ।
तथा विधानं क्रियतां समर्थाः करणेष्विह ।। 16 ।।

तथेति च ततः सर्वे मंत्रिणः प्रत्यपूजयन् ।
पार्थिवेन्द्रस्य तद्वाक्यं यथाज्ञप्तमकुर्वत ।। 17 ।।

ततो द्विजास्ते धर्मज्ञमस्तुवन्पार्थिवर्षभम् ।
अनुज्ञातास्ततः सर्वे पुनर्जग्मुर्यथागतम् ।। 18 ।।

गतानां तु द्विजातीनां मंत्रिणस्तान्नराधिपः ।
विसर्जयित्वा तं वेश्म प्रविवेश महाद्युतिः ।। 19 ।।

Canto V (Canto XII of the present *Rāmāyaṇa*)

पुनः प्राप्ते वसन्ते तुपूर्णः संवत्सरोऽभवत् ।
अभिबाद्य वसिष्ठं च न्यायतः प्रतिपूज्य च ।। 1 ।।

अब्रवीत्प्रश्रितं वाक्यं प्रसवार्थं द्विजोत्तमम् ।
यज्ञं में क्रियतां विप्र यथोक्तं मुनिपुंगव ।। 2 ।।

यथा न विघ्नः क्रियते यज्ञांगेषु विधीययाम् ।
भवान् स्निग्धः सुहृन्मह्यं गुरुश्च परमो भवान्।। 3 ।।

वोढव्यो भवता चैव भारो यज्ञस्य चोद्यतः ।
तथेति च स राजानमब्रवीद्द्विजसत्तमः ।। 4 ।।

करिष्ये सर्वमेवैतद्भवता यत्समर्थितम् ।
वतोऽब्रवीद्द्विजान् वृद्धान् यज्ञकर्मसु निष्ठितान् ।। 5 ।।

स्थापत्ये निष्ठितांश्चैव वृद्धान् परमधार्मिकान् ।
कर्मान्तिकान् शिल्पकारान् वर्धकीन्खनकानपि ।। 6 ।।

गणकाञ्शिल्पिनश्चैव तथैव नटनर्तकान् ।
तथा शुचीञ्शास्त्रविदः पुरुषान् सुबहुश्रुतान् ।। 7 ।।

गज्ञकर्म समीहन्तां भवन्तो राजशासनात् ।
इष्टका वहुस्त्राहस्त्री शीघ्रमानीयतामिति ।। 8 ।।

औपकार्याः क्रियन्तां च राज्ञां बहुगुणान्विताः ।
ब्राह्मणावसथाश्चैव कर्तव्याः शतशः शुभाः ।। 9 ।।

भक्ष्यान्नपानैर्बहुभिः समुपेताः सुनिष्ठिताः ।
तथा पौरजनस्यापि कर्तव्या बहुविस्तराः ।। 10 ।।

आवासा बहुभक्ष्या वै सर्वकामैरूपस्थिताः
वथा जानपदस्यापि जनस्य बहुशोभनम् ।। 11 ।।

दातव्यमन्नं विधिवत्सत्कृत्य न तु लीलया ।
सर्ववर्णा यथा पूजां प्राप्नुवन्ति सुसत्कृताः ।। 12 ।।

न चावज्ञा प्रयोक्तव्या कामक्रोधवशादपि ।
यज्ञकर्मसु येऽव्यग्राः पुरुषाः शिल्पिनस्तथा ।। 13 ।।

वेषामपि विशेषेण पूजा कार्या यथाक्रमम् ।
यथा सर्वं सुविहितं न किंचित्परिहीयते ।। 14 ।।

तथा भवन्तः कुर्वन्तु प्रीतिस्निग्धेन चेतसा ।
ततः सर्वे समागत्य वसिष्ठमिदमब्रुवन् ।। 15 ।।

यथोक्तं तत्करिष्यामो न किंचित् परिहास्यते ।
ततः सुमंत्रमाहूय वसिष्ठो वाक्यमब्रवीत् ।। 16 ।।

निमंत्रयस्व नृपतीन् पृथिव्यां ये च धार्मिकाः ।
ब्राह्मणान्क्षत्रियान्वैश्यान्शूद्रांश्चैव सहस्रशः ।। 17 ।।

समानयस्व सत्कृत्य सर्वदेशेषु मानवान् ।
मिथिलाधिपतिं शूरं जनकं सत्यविक्रमम् ।। 18 ।।

निष्ठितं सर्वशास्त्रेषु तथा वेदेषु निष्ठितम् ।
तमानय महाभागं स्वयमेव सुसत्कृतम् ।
पूर्वसंबन्धिनं ज्ञात्वा ततः पूर्वं ब्रवोमि ते ।। 19 ।।

तथा काशिपतिं स्निग्धं सततं प्रियवादिनम् ।
सद्वृत्तं देवसंकाशं स्वयमेवानयस्व ह ।। 20 ।।

तथा केकयराजानं वृद्धं परमधार्मिकम् ।
श्वशुरं राजसिंहस्य सपुत्रं तमिहानय ।। 21 ।।

अंगेश्वरं महाभागं रोमपादं सुसत्कृतम् ।
वयस्यं राजसिंहस्य तमानय यशस्विनम् ।। 22 ।।

प्राचीनान् सिन्धुसौवीरान्सौराष्ट्रेयांश्च पार्थिवान् ।
दाक्षिणात्यान्नरेन्द्रांश्च समस्तानानयस्त्र ह ।। 23 ।।

सन्ति स्निग्धाश्च ये चान्ये राजानः पृथिवीतले ।
तानानय यथा क्षिप्रं सानुगान्सहबान्धवानू ।। 24 ।।

वसिष्ठवाक्यं तच्छ्रुत्वा सुमंत्रस्त्वरितस्तदा ।
व्यादिशत्पुरुषांस्तत्र राज्ञामानयने शुभान् ।। 25 ।।

स्वयमेव हि धर्मात्या प्रययौ मुनिशासनात् ।
सुमंत्रस्त्वरितो भूत्वा समानेतुं महीक्षितः ।। 26 ।।

ते च कर्मान्तिकाः सर्वे वसिष्ठाय च धीमते ।
सर्वं निवेदयन्ति सम यज्ञे यदुपकल्पितम् ।। 27 ।।

ततः प्रीतो द्विज श्रेष्ठस्तान्सर्वान्पुनरब्रवीत् ।
अवज्ञया न दातव्यं कस्यचिल्लीलयापि वा ।
अवज्ञया कृतं हन्याद्दातारं नात्र संशयः ।। 28 ।।

ततः कैश्चिदहोरात्रैरुपयाता महीक्षितः ।
बहूनि रत्नान्यादाय राज्ञो दशरथस्य ह ।। 29 ।।

ततो वसिष्ठः सुप्रीतो राजानमिदमब्रवीत् ।
उपयाता नरव्याघ्र राजानस्तवं शासनात् ।। 30 ।।

मयापि सत्कृताः सर्वे यथार्हं राजसन्तमा ।
यज्ञियं च कृतं राजन् पुरुषैः सुसमाहितैः ।। 31 ।।

निर्यातु च भवान्यष्टुं यज्ञायतनमन्तिकात् ।
सर्वकामैरुपहृतैरुपेतं वैं समन्ततः ।। 32 ।।

तथा वसिष्ठवचनादृष्यशृंगस्य चोभयोः ।
शुभे दिवसनक्षत्रे निर्यातो जगतीपतिः ।। 33 ।।

ततो वसिष्ठप्रमुखाः सर्व एव द्विजोत्तमाः ।
ऋष्यशृंगं पुरस्कृत्य यज्ञकर्मारभंस्तदा ।। 34 ।।

Canto VI (Canto XIII of the present *Rāmāyaṇa*)

अथ संवत्सरे पूर्णे तस्मिन् प्राप्ते तुरंगमे ।
सरय्वाश्चोत्तरे तीरे राज्ञो यज्ञोऽभ्यवर्तत ।। 1 ।।

ऋष्यशृंगं पुरस्कृत्य कर्म चक्रुर्द्विजर्षभाः ।
अश्वमेधे महायज्ञे राज्ञोऽस्य सुमहात्मनः ।। 2 ।।

कर्म कुर्वन्ति विधिवद् याजका वेदपारगाः ।
यथाविधि यथान्यायं परिक्रामन्ति शास्त्रतः ।। 3 ।।

प्रवर्ग्यं शास्त्रतः कृत्वा तथैवोपसदं द्विजाः ।
चक्रुश्च विधिवत्सर्वमधिकं कर्म शास्त्रतः ।। 4 ।।

अभिपूज्य ततो हृष्टाः सर्वे चक्रुर्यथाविधि ।
प्रातःसवनपूर्वाणि कर्माणि मुनिपुंगवाः ।। 5 ।।

न चाहुतमभूत्तत्र स्खलितं वापि किंचन ।
दृश्यते ब्रह्मवत्सर्वं क्षेममुक्तं हि चक्रिरे ।। 6 ।।

न तेष्वहःसु श्रान्तो वा क्षुधितो वापि दृश्यते ।
नाविद्वान् ब्राह्मणस्तत्र नाशतानुचरस्तथा ।। 7 ।।

ब्राह्मणा भुञ्जते नित्यं नाथवन्तश्च भुञ्जते ।
तापसा भुञ्जते चापि श्रमणा भुञ्जते तथा ।। 8 ।।

वृद्धाश्च व्याधिताश्चैव स्त्रियो बालास्तथैव च ।
अनिशं भुञ्जमानानां न तृप्तिरूपलभ्यते ।। 9 ।।

दीयतां दीयतामन्नं वासांसि विविधानि च ।
इति संचोदितास्तत्र तथा चक्रुरनेकशः ।। 10 ।।

अन्नकूटाश्च बहवो दृश्यन्ते पर्वतोपमाः ।
दिवसे दिवसे तत्र सिद्धस्य विधिवत्तदा ।। 11 ।।

अन्न हि विधिवत्स्वादु प्रशंसन्ति द्विजर्षभाः ।
अहो तृप्ताःस्म भद्रं ते इति शुश्राव राघवः ।। 12 ।।

स्वलंकृताश्च पुरुषा ब्राह्मणान्पर्यवेषयन् ।
उपासते च तानन्ये सुमृष्टमणिकुण्डलाः ।। 13 ।।

कर्मान्तरे तदा विप्रा हेतुवादान्बहूनपिं ।
प्राहुः सुवाग्मिनो धीराः परस्परजिगीषया ।। 14 ।।

दिवसे दिवसे तत्र संस्तरे कुशला द्विजाः ।
सर्वकर्माणि चक्रुस्ते यथाशास्त्रं प्रचोदिताः ।। 15 ।।

नाषडंगविंदत्रासीन्नाव्रतो नाबहुश्रुतः ।
सदस्यस्तस्य वै राज्ञो नावादकुशलो द्विजः ।। 16 ।।

प्राप्ते यूपोच्छ्रये तस्मिन्षड् बैल्वाः खादिरास्तथा ।
तावन्तो बिल्वसहिताः पर्णिनश्च तथापरे ।। 17 ।।

श्लेष्मातकमयो दिष्टो देवदारुमयस्तथा ।
द्वावेव तत्र विहितौ बाहुव्यस्तपरिग्रहौ ।। 18 ।।

कारिताः सर्व एवैते शास्त्रज्ञैर्यज्ञकोविदैः ।
शोभार्थं तस्य यज्ञस्य काञ्चनालंकृता भवन् ।। 19।।

विन्यस्ता विधिवत्सर्वे शिल्पिभिः सुकृता दृढाः ।
अष्टास्त्रयः सर्व एव श्लक्ष्णारूपसमन्विताः ।। 20 ।।

आच्छादितास्ते वासोभिः पुष्पैर्गन्धैश्च भूषिताः ।
सप्तर्षयो दीप्तिमन्तो विराजन्ते यथा दिवि ।। 21 ।।

इष्टकाश्च यथान्थायं कारिताश्च प्रमाणतः ।
चितोग्निर्ब्राह्मणैस्तत्र कुशलैः शुल्वकर्मणि ।। 22 ।।

गरूडो रुक्मपक्षो वै त्रिगुणोऽष्टादशात्मकः ।
नियुक्तास्तत्र पशवस्तत्तदुद्दिश्य दैवतम् ।। 23 ।।

उरगाः पक्षिणश्चैव यथाशास्त्रं प्रचोदिताः ।
शामित्रे तु हयस्तत्र तथा जलचराश्ध ये ।। 24 ।।

ऋत्विग्भिः सर्वमेवैतन्नियुक्तं शास्त्रतस्तदा ।
पशूनां त्रिशतं तत्र यूपेषु नियतं तदा ।
अश्वरत्नोत्तमं तस्य राज्ञो दशरथस्य ह ।। 25 ।।

कौसल्या तं हयं तत्र परिचर्य समन्ततः ।
कृपाणैः विशशासैनं त्रिभिः परमया मुदा ।। 26 ।।

पतत्रिणा तदा सार्धं सुस्थितेन च चेतसा ।
अवसद्रजनीमेकां कौसल्या धर्मकाम्यया ।। 27 ।।

होतोध्वर्युस्तथोद्गाता हयेन समयोजयन् ।
महिष्या परिवृत्त्याथ बावातामपरां तथा ।। 28 ।।

पतत्रिणस्तस्य वपामुद्धृत्य नियतेन्द्रियः ।
ऋत्विक्परमसंपन्नः श्रपयामास शास्त्रतः ।। 29 ।।

धूमगन्धं वपायास्तु जिघ्रति स्म नराधिपः ।
यथाकालं यथान्यायं निर्णुदन्पापमात्मनः ।। 30 ।।

हयस्व याानि चांगानि तानि सर्वाणि ब्राह्मणाः ।
अग्नौ प्रास्यन्ति विधिवत्समस्ताः षोडशर्त्विजः ।। 31 ।।

प्लक्षशाखासु यज्ञानामन्येषां क्रियते हविः ।
अश्वमेघस्य चैकस्य वैतसो भाग इष्यते ।। 32 ।।

त्र्यहोऽश्वमेधः संख्यातः कल्पसूत्रेण ब्राह्मणैः ।
चतुष्टोममहस्तस्य प्रथमं परिकल्पितम् ।। 33 ।।

उक्थ्यं द्वितीयं संख्यातमतिरात्रं तथोत्तरम् ।
कारितास्तत्र ब्रहवो विहिताः शास्त्रदर्शनात् ।। 34 ।।

ज्योतिष्टोमायुषी चैव अतिरात्रौ च निर्मितौ ।
अभिजिद्विश्वजिच्चैव अप्तोर्यामो महाक्रतुः ।। 35 ।।

प्राचीं होत्रे ददौ राजा दिशं स्वकुलवर्धनः ।
अध्वर्यवे प्रतीचीं तु ब्रह्मणे दक्षिणां दिशम् ।। 36 ।।

उद्गात्रे तु तथोदीचीं दक्षिणैषा विनिर्मिता ।
अश्वमेधे महायज्ञे स्वयं मुविहिते पुरा ।। 37 ।।

क्रतुं समाप्य तु तदा न्यायतः पुरुषर्षमः ।
ऋत्विग्भ्यो हि ददौ राजा धरां तां क्रतुवर्धनः ।। 38 ।।

ऋत्विजस्त्वब्रुवन्सर्वे राजानं गतकल्मषभ् ।
भवानेव महीं कृत्स्नामेको रक्षितुमर्हति ।। 39 ।।

न भूम्या कार्यमस्माकं न हि शक्ताःस्म पालने ।
रताः स्वाध्यायकरणे वयं नित्यं हि भूमिप ।
निष्क्रयं किंचिदेवेह प्रयच्छतु भवानिति ।। 40 ।।

गवां शतसहस्त्राणि दश तेभ्यो ददौ नृपः ।
दशकोटिं सुवर्णस्य रजतस्य चतुर्गुणम् ।। 41 ।।

ऋत्विजस्तु ततः सर्वे प्रददुः सहिता वसु ।
ऋष्यशृंगाय मुनये वसिष्ठाय च धीमते ।। 42 ।।

ततस्ते न्यायतः कृत्वा प्रविभागं द्विजोत्तमाः ।
सुप्रीतमनसः सर्वे प्रत्यूचुर्मुदिता भृशम् ।। 43 ।।

ततः प्रीतमना राजा प्राप्य यज्ञमनुत्तमम् ।
पापापहं स्वर्नयनं दुस्तरं पार्थिवर्षभैः ।। 44 ।।

Canto VII (Canto XVII of the present *Rāmāyaṇa*)

निवृत्ते नु क्रतौ तस्मिन्हयमेधे महात्मनः ।
प्रतिगृह्य सुरा भागान् प्रतिजग्मुर्यथागतम् ।। 1 ।।

समाप्तदीक्षानियमः पत्नीगणसभन्वितः ।
प्रविवेश पुरीं राजा सभृत्यबलवाहनः ।। 2 ।।

यथार्हं पूजितास्तेन राज्ञा वै पृथिवीश्वराः ।
मुदिताः प्रत्ययुर्देशान्प्रणम्य मुनिपुंगवम् ।। 3 ।।

गतेषु पृथिवीशेषु राजा दशरथः पुनः ।
प्रविवेश पुरीं श्रीमान्पुरस्कृत्य द्विजोत्तमान् ।। 4 ।।

शान्तया प्रययौ सार्धमृष्यशृंगः सुपूजितः ।
अन्वीयमानो राज्ञाथ सानुयात्रेंण धीमता ।। 5 ।।

एवं विसृज्य तान्सर्वान्राजा संपूर्णमानसः ।
उवास सुखितस्तत्र पुत्रोत्पत्तिं विचिन्तयन् ।। 6 ।।

ततो यज्ञे समाप्ते तु ऋतूनां षट् समत्ययुः ।
ततश्च द्वादशे मासे चैत्रे नावमिके तिथौ ।
कौसल्याजनयद्रामं दिव्यलक्षणसंयुतन् ।। 7 ।।

कौसल्या शुशुभे तेन पुत्रेणामिततेजसा ।
यथा वरेण देवानामदितिर्वज्रपाणिना ।। 8 ।।

भरतो नाम केंकेय्थां ज़ज्ञे सत्यपराक्रमः ।
अथ लक्ष्मणशत्रुघ्नौ सुमित्राजनयत्सुतौ ।। 9 ।।

राज्ञः पुत्रा महात्मानश्चत्यारो जज्ञिरे पृथक् ।
गुणवन्तोऽनुरूपाश्च रुच्या प्रोष्ठपदोपमाः ।। 10 ।।

अतीत्यैकादशाहं तु नामकर्म तथाकरोत् ।
ज्येष्ठं रामं महात्मानं भरतं कैकयीसुतम् ।। 11 ।।

सौमित्रिं लक्ष्मणमिति शत्रुघ्नमपरं तथा ।
वसिष्ठः परमप्रीतो नामानि कृतवांस्तदा ।
तेषां जन्मक्रियादीनि सर्वकर्माण्यकारयत् ।। 12 ।।

तेषां केतुरिव ज्येष्ठो रामो रतिकरः पितुः ।
बभूव भूयो भूतानां स्वयंमूरिव संमतः ।। 13 ।।

सर्वे वेदविदः शूराः सर्वे लोकहिते रताः ।
सर्वे ज्ञानोपसंपन्नाः सर्वे समुदिता गुणैः ।। 14 ।।

तेषयपिं महातेजा रामः सत्यपराक्रमः ।
बाल्यात्प्रभृति सुस्निग्धो लक्ष्मणो लक्ष्मिवर्धनः ।। 15 ।।

रामस्य लोकरायस्य भ्रातुर्ज्येष्ठस्य नित्यशः ।
सर्वप्रियकरस्तस्य रामस्यापि शरीरतः ।। 16 ।।

लक्ष्मणो लक्ष्मिसंपन्नो बहिःप्राण इवापरः ।
न च तेन विना निद्रां लभते पुरुषोत्तमः ।
मृष्टमन्नमुपानीतमश्नाति न हि तं विना ।। 17 ।।

यदा हि हयमारूढो मृगयां याति राघवः ।
तदैनं पृष्ठतोऽभ्येनि सधनुः परिपालयन् ।। 18 ।।

भरतस्यापि शत्रुघ्नो लक्ष्मणवरजो हि सः ।
प्राणैः प्रियतरो नित्यं तस्य चासीत्तथा प्रियः ।। 19 ।।

स चतुर्भिर्महाभागैः पुत्रैः दशरथः प्रियैः ।
वभूव परमप्रीतो देवैरिव पितामहः ।। 20 ।।

Canto VIII (Particulars of the corresponding Cantos and verses of the present *Rāmāyaṇa* have been noted against the stanzas)

तदा कुशिकपुत्रं तु धनुष्पाणी स्वलंकृतौ ।
बद्धगोधांगुलित्राणौ खड्गवन्तौ महाद्युती ।।
कुमारौ चारुवपुषौ भ्रातरौ रामलक्ष्मणौ ।
अनुयातौ श्रिया दीप्तौ शोभयेतामनिन्दितौ ।। XXI. 8 and 8 a

तौ प्रयातौ महावीर्यौ त्रिपथगां नदीम् ।
ददृशाते ततस्तत्र सरय्वाः संगमे शुभे ।। XXII. 5

अथ तां रजनीं तत्र कृतार्थौ रामलक्ष्मणौ ।
ऊषतुर्मुदितौ वीरौ प्रहृष्टेनान्तरात्मना ।। XXX. 1

उत्तरं तीरमासाद्य संपूज्यर्षिगणं ततः ।
गंगातीरे निविष्टास्ते विशालां ददृशुः पुरीम् ।।
ततो मुनिवरस्तूर्ण जगाम सहराघवः ।
विशालां नगरीं रम्यां दिव्यां स्वर्गोपमां तदा ।। XLIV. 8 and 9

ततः परमसत्कारं सुमतेः प्राप्य राघवौ ।
उष्य तत्र निशामेकां जग्मतुर्मिथिलां ततः ।।
तां दृष्ट्वा मुनयः सर्वे जनकस्य पुरीं शुभाम् ।
साधु साध्विति शंसन्तो मिथिलां समपूजयन् ।। XLVII. 9 and 10.

रामस्तु मुनिशार्दूलमुवाच सहलक्ष्मणः ।

साध्वी यज्ञसमृद्धिर्हि जनकस्य महात्मनः ।।

बहूनीह सहस्राणि नानादेशनिवासिनाम् ।
ब्राह्मणानाँ महाभाग वेदाध्ययनशालिनाम् ।।
अथ राजा मुनिश्रेष्ठं कृतांजलिरभाषत ।
आसने भागवानास्तां सहैभिर्मुनिसत्तमैः ।। IL. 2, 3, and 10

तमर्चयित्वा धर्मात्मा शास्त्रदृष्टेन कर्मणा ।
राघवौ च महात्मानौ तदा वाक्यमुवाच ह ।।

भगवन् स्वागतं तेऽस्तु किं करोमि तवानघ ।
भगवानाज्ञापयतु मामाज्ञाप्यो भवता ह्यहम् ।।
एवमुक्तः स धर्मात्मा जनकेन महात्मना ।
प्रत्युवाच मुनिर्वीरं वाक्यं वाक्यविशारदः ।।
पुत्रौ दशरथस्येमौ क्षत्रियौ लोकविश्रुतौ ।
द्रष्टुकामौ धनुः श्रेष्ठं यदेत्त्वयि तिष्ठति ।।
एतद् दर्शय भद्रं ते कृतकामौ नृपात्मजौ ।
दर्शनादस्य धनुषो यथेष्टं प्रतियास्यतः ।। LXV.2-6

Canto IX (Canto LXVI of the present *Rāmāyaṇa*)

ततः स राजा जनकः सचिवान्व्यादिदेश ह ।
धनुरानीयतां दिव्यं गन्धमाल्यविभूषितम् ।। 1 ।।

जनकेन समादिष्टाः सचिवाः प्राविशन्पुरीम् ।
तद्धनुः पुरतः कृत्वा निर्जग्मुः पार्थिवाज्ञया ।। 2 ।।

पश्यतां नृसहस्राणां बहूनां रघुनन्दनः ।
आरोपयत्स धर्मात्मा सलीलमिव तद्धनुः ।। 3 ।।

आरोपयित्वा मौर्वी च पूरयामास वीर्यवान् ।
तद्बभंज धनुर्मध्ये नरश्रेष्ठो महायशाः ।। 4 ।।

तस्य शब्दो महानासीन्निर्घातसमनिस्वनः ।
भूमिकम्पश्च सुमहान्पर्वतस्येव दीर्यतः ।। 5 ।।

निपेतुश्च नराः सर्वे तेन शब्देन मोहिताः ।
वर्जयित्वा मुनिवरं राजानं तौ च राघवौ ।। 6 ।।

प्रत्याश्वस्ते जने तस्मिन्राजा विगतसाध्वसः ।
उवाच प्राञ्जलिर्वाक्यं वाक्यज्ञो मुनिपुंगवम् ।। 7 ।।

भगवन् दृष्टवीर्यो मे रामो दशरथात्मजः ।
अत्यद्भुतमचिन्त्यं च अतर्कितमिदं मया ।। 8 ।।

जनकानां कुले कीर्तिमाहरिष्यति मे सुता ।
सीता भर्तारमासाद्य रामं दशरथात्मजम् ।। 9 ।।

मम सत्या प्रतिज्ञा च वीर्यशुल्केति कौशिक।
सीता प्राणैर्बहुमता देया रामाय मे सुता ।। 10 ।।

भवतोऽनुमते ब्रह्मञ्शीघ्रं गच्छन्तु मन्त्रिणः ।
मम कौशिक भद्रं ते अयोध्यां त्वरिता रथैः ।। 11 ।।

राजानं प्रश्रितैवाक्यैरानयन्तु पुरं मम ।
प्रदानं वीर्यशुल्कायाः कथयन्तु च सर्वशः ।। 12 ।।

मुनिगुप्तौ च काकुत्स्थौ कथयन्तु नृपाय वै ।
प्रीयमाणं च राजानमानयन्तु सुशीघ्रगाः ।। 13 ।।

कौशिकश्च तथेत्याह राजा चाभाष्य मन्त्रिणः ।
अयोध्यां प्रेषयामास धर्मात्मा कृतशासनान् ।। 14 ।।

Canto X (Canto LXVII of the present *Rāmāyaṇa*)

जनकेन समादिष्टा दूतास्ते क्लान्तवाहनाः
त्रिरात्रमुषिता मार्गे तेऽयोध्यां प्राविशन्पुरीम् ।। 1 ।।

ते राजवचनाद्दूता राजवेश्म प्रवेशिताः ।
ददृशुर्देवसंकाशं वृद्धं दशरथं नृपम् ।। 2 ।।

वद्धाञ्जलिपुटाः सर्वे दूता विगतसाध्वसाः ।
राजानं प्रयता वाक्यमब्रुवन्मधुराक्षरम् ।। 3 ।।

मैथिलो जनको राजा साग्निहोत्रपुरस्कृतः ।
कुशलं चाव्ययं चैव सोपाध्यायपुरोहितम् ।। 4 ।।

मुहुर्मुहुर्मधुरया स्नेहसंयुक्तया गिरा ।
जनकस्त्वां महाराज पृच्छते सपुरःसरम् ।। 5 ।।

पृष्ट्वा कुशलमव्यग्रं वैदेहो मिथिलाधिपः ।
कौशिकानुमते वाक्यं भवन्तमिदमब्रवीत् ।। 6 ।।

पूर्वं प्रतिज्ञा विदिता वीर्यशुल्का ममात्मजा ।
राजानश्च कृतामर्षा निर्वीर्या विमुखीकृताः ।। 7 ।।

तच्च राजन्धनुर्दिव्यं मध्ये भग्नं महात्मना ।
रामेण हि महाराज महत्यां जनसंसदि ।। 8 ।।

अस्मै देया मया सीता वीर्यशुल्का महात्मने ।
प्रतिज्ञां तर्तुमिच्छामि तदनुज्ञातुमर्हसि ।। 9 ।।

सोपाध्यायो महाराज पुरोहितपुरस्कृतः।
शीघ्रमागच्छ भद्रं ते द्रष्टुमर्हसि राघवौ ।। 10 ।।

प्रीतिं च मम राजेन्द्र निर्वर्तयितुमर्हसि ।
पुत्रयोरुभयोरेब प्रीतिं त्वममि लप्स्यसे ।। 11 ।।

दूतवाक्यं तु तच्छ्रुत्वा राजा परमहर्षितः ।
वसिष्ठं वामदेवं च मन्त्रिणोऽन्यांश्च सोऽब्रवीत् ।। 12 ।।

गुप्ताः कुशिकपुत्रेण कौसल्यानन्दवर्धनः ।
लक्ष्मणेन सह भ्रात्रा विदेहेषु वसत्यसौ ।। 13 ।।

दृष्टवीर्यस्तु काकुत्स्थो जनकेन महात्मना ।
संप्रदानं सुतायास्तु राघवे कर्तुमिच्छति ।। 14 ।।

यदि वो रोचते वृत्तं जनकस्य महात्मनः ।
पुरीं गच्छामहे शीघ्रं मा भूत्कालस्य पर्ययः ।। 15 ।।

मंत्रिणो बाढमित्याहुः सह सर्वैर्महर्षिभिः ।
सुप्रीतश्चाब्रवीद्राजा श्वो यात्रेति स मन्त्रिणः ।। 16 ।।

मन्त्रिणस्तु नरेन्द्रस्य रात्रिं परमसत्कृताः ।
ऊषुः प्रमुदिताः सर्वे गुणैः सर्वैः समन्विताः ।। 17 ।।

Canto XI (Canto LXVIII of the present *Rāmāyaṇa*)

ततो रात्र्यां व्यतीतायां सोपाध्यायः सबान्धवः ।
राजा दशरथो हृष्टः सुमन्त्रमिदमब्रवीत् ।। 1 ।।

अद्य सर्वे धनाध्यक्षा धनमादाघ पुष्कलम् ।
व्रजन्त्वग्रे सुविहिता नानारत्नसमन्विताः ।। 2 ।।

चतुरंगबलं चापि शीघ्रं निर्यातु सर्वशः ।
ममाज्ञासमकालं च यानयुग्मयमनुत्तमम् ।। 3 ।।

वसिष्ठो वामदेवश्च जाबालिरथ काश्यपः ।
मार्कण्डेयश्च दीर्घायुर्ऋषिः कात्यायनस्तथा ।। 4 ।।

एते द्विजाः प्रयान्त्वग्रे स्यन्दनं योजयस्व मे ।
यथा कालात्ययो न स्याद्दूता हि त्वरयन्ति माम् ।। 5 ।।

बचनाच्च नरेन्द्रस्य सा सेना चतुरंगिणी ।
राजानं ऋषिभिः सार्धं व्रजन्तं पृष्ठतोऽन्वगात् ।। 6 ।।

गत्वा चतुरहं मार्गं विदेहानभ्युपेयिवान् ।
राजा तु जनकः श्रीमादञ्श्रुत्वा पूजामकल्पयत् ।। 7 ।।

ततो राजानमासाद्य वृद्धं दशरथं नृपम् ।
जनको मुदितो राजा हर्ष च परमं ययौ ।
उवाच च नरश्रेष्ठो नरश्रेष्ठं मुदान्वितम् ।। 8 ।।

स्वागतं ते महाराज दिष्ट्या प्राप्तोऽसि राघव ।
पुत्रघोरुभयोः प्रीतिं लप्स्यसे वीर्यनिर्जिताम् ।। 9 ।।

दिष्ट्या प्राप्तो महातेजा वसिष्ठो भगवानृषिः
सह सर्वैर्द्विजश्रेष्ठैर्देवैरिव शतक्रतुः ।। 10 ।।

दिष्ट्या मे निर्जिता विघ्ना दिष्ट्या मे पूजितं कुलम् ।
राघवैः सह संबन्धाद्वीर्यश्रेष्ठैर्महात्मभिः ।। 11 ।।

श्वः प्रभाते नरेन्द्रेन्द्र निर्वर्तयितुमर्हसि ।
यज्ञस्यान्ते नरश्रेष्ठ विवाहमृषिसंमतम् ।। 12 ।।

तस्य तद्वचनं श्रुत्वा ऋषिमध्ये नराधिपः ।
वाक्यं वाक्यविदां श्रेष्ठः प्रत्युवाच महीपतिम् ।। 13 ।।

प्रतिग्रहो दातृवशः श्रुतमेतन्मया पुरा ।
यथा वक्ष्यसि धर्मज्ञ तत्करिष्यामहे वयम् ।। 14 ।।

तद्धर्मिष्ठं यशस्यं च वचनं सत्यवादिनः ।
श्रुत्वा विदेहाधिपति परं विस्मयमागतः ।। 15 ।।

ततः सर्वे मुनिगणाः परस्परसमागमे ।
हर्षेण महता युक्तास्तां निशामवसन्सुखम् ।। 16 ।।

राजा च राघवौ पुत्रौ निशाभ्य परिहर्षितः ।
उवास परमप्रीतो जनकेन सुपूजितः ।। 17 ।।

जनकोऽपि महातेजाः क्रिया धर्मेण तत्त्ववित् ।
यज्ञस्य च सुनाभ्यां च कृत्वा रात्रिमुवास ह ।। 18 ।।

Canto XII (Canto LXIX of the present *Rāmāyaṇa*)

ततः प्रभाते जनकः कृतकर्मा महर्षिभिः ।
उवाच वाक्यं वाक्यज्ञः शतानन्दं पुरोहितम् ।। 1 ।।

भ्राता मम महातेजा यवीयानतिधार्मिकः ।
कुशध्वज इति ख्यातः पुरीमध्यवसच्छुभाम ।। 2 ।।

बार्याफलकपर्यन्तां पिबन्निक्षुमतीं नदीम् ।
सांकाश्यां पुण्यसंकाशां विमानमिव पुष्पकम् ।। 3 ।।

तमहं द्रष्टुमिच्छामि यज्ञगोप्ता स मे मतः ।
प्रीतिं सोऽपि महातेजा इमां भोक्ता मया सह ।। 4 ।।

शासनात्तु नरेन्द्रस्य प्रययुः शीघ्रवाजिभिः ।
समानेतुं नरव्याघ्रं विष्णुमिन्द्राज्ञया यथा ।। 5 ।।

आज्ञया तु नरेन्द्रस्य आजगाम कुशध्वजः ।। 6 ।।

स ददर्श महात्मानं जनकं धर्मवत्सलम् ।
सोऽभिवाद्य शतानन्दं राजानं चापि धार्मिकम् ।। 7 ।।

राजार्हं परमं दिव्यमासनं चाध्यरोहत ।
उपविष्टावुभौ तौ तु भ्रातरावमितौजसौ ।। 8 ।।

प्रेषयामासतुर्वीरौ मन्त्रिश्रेष्ठं सुदामनम् ।
गच्छ मन्त्रिपते शीघ्रमैक्ष्वाकममितप्रभम ।
आत्मजैः सह दुर्धर्षमानयस्व समन्त्रिणम् ।। 9 ।।

औपकार्यां स गत्वा तु रघूणां कुलवर्धनम् ।
ददर्श शिरसा चैनमभिवाद्येदमब्रवीत् ।। 10 ।।

अयोध्याधिपते वीर वैदेहो मिथिलाधिपः ।
स त्वां द्रष्टुं व्यवसितः सोपाध्यायपुरोहितम् ।। 11 ।।

मंत्रिश्रेष्ठवचः श्रुत्वा राजा सर्षिगणस्तदा ।
सबन्धुरागमत्तत्र जनको यत्र वर्तते ।। 12 ।।

स राजा मन्त्रिसहितः सोपाध्यायः सबान्धवः ।
वाक्यं वाक्यविदां श्रेष्ठो वैदेहमिदमब्रवीत् ।। 13 ।।

विदितं ते महाराज इक्ष्वाकुकुलदैवतम् ।
वक्ता सर्वेषु कृत्येषु वसिष्ठो भगवानृषिः ।। 14 ।।

तूष्णींभूते दशरथे वसिष्ठो भगवानृषिः ।
उवाच वाक्यं वाक्यज्ञो वैदेहं सपुरोहितम् ।। 15 ।।

रामलक्ष्मणयोरर्थे त्वत्सुते वरये नृप ।
सदृशाभ्यां नरश्रेष्ठ सदृशे दातुमर्हसि ।। 16 ।।

Canto XIII (Canto LXX of the present *Rāmāyaṇa*)

एवं ब्रुवाणं जनकः प्रत्युवाच कृताञ्जलिः ।
श्रोतुमर्हसि भद्रं ते कुलं नः कीर्तितं परम् ।। 1 ।।

प्रदाने हि मुनिश्रेष्ठ कुलं निरवशेषतः ।
वक्तव्यं कुलजातेन तन्निबोध महामुने ।। 2 ।।

राजाभूत्त्रिषुलोकेषु विश्रुतः स्वेन कर्मणा ।
निमिः परमधर्मात्मा सर्वसत्त्ववतां वरः ।। 3 ।।

तस्य पुत्रो मिथिर्नाम जनको मिथिपुत्रकः ।
प्रथमो जनको नाम जनकादप्युदावसुः ।। 4 ।।

उदावसोस्तु धर्मात्मा जातो वै नन्दिवर्धनः ।
नन्दिवर्धनपुत्रस्तु सुकेतुर्नाम नामतः ।। 5 ।।

सुकेतोरपि धर्मात्मा देवरातो महाबलः ।
देवरातस्य राजर्षेर्बृहद्रथ इति श्रुतः ।। 6 ।।

बृहद्रथस्य शूरोऽभून्महावीरः प्रतापवान् ।
महावीरस्य धृतिमान्सुधृतिः सत्यविक्रमः ।। 7 ।।

सुधृतेरपि धर्मात्मा धृष्टकेतुः सुधार्मिकः ।
धृष्टकेतोस्तु राजर्षेर्हर्यश्च इति विश्रुतः ।। 8 ।।

हर्धश्वस्य मरुः पुत्रो मरोः पुत्रः प्रतीन्धकः ।
प्रतीन्धकस्य धर्मात्मा राजा कीर्तिरथः सुतः ।। 9 ।।

पुत्रः कीर्तिरथस्यामि देवमीढ इति स्मृतः ।
देबमीढस्य विबुधो विबुधस्य महीध्रकः ।। 10 ।।

महीध्रकसुतो राजा कीर्तिरातो महाबलः ।
कीर्तिरातस्य राजर्षेर्महारोमा व्यजायत ।। 11 ।।

महारोम्णस्तु धर्मात्मा स्वर्णरोमा व्यजायत ।
स्वर्णरोम्णस्तु राजर्षेर्ह्रस्वरोमा व्यजायत ।। 12 ।।

तस्य पुत्रद्वयं जज्ञे धर्मज्ञस्य महात्मनः ।
ज्येष्ठोऽहमनुजो भ्राता मम वीरः कुशध्वजः ।। 13 ।।

मां तु ज्येष्ठं पिता राज्ये सोऽभिषिच्य नराधिपः ।
कुशध्वजं समावेश्य भारं मयि बनं गतः ।। 14 ।।

बृद्धे पितरि स्वर्याते धर्मेण धुरमावहम् ।
भ्रातरं देवसंकाशं स्नेहात्पश्यन्कुशध्वजम् ।। 15 ।।

कस्यचित्त्वथ कालस्य सांकाश्यादगमत्पुरात् ।
सुधन्वा वीर्यवान्राजा मिथिलामवरोधकः ।। 16 ।।

स च मे प्रेषयाभास शैवं धनुरनुत्तमम् ।
सीता कन्या च पद्माक्षी मह्यं वै दीयतामिति ।। 17 ।।

तस्याप्रदानाद्ब्रह्मर्षे युद्धभासीन् मया सह ।
स हतोऽभिमुखो राजा सुधन्वा तु मया रणे ।। 18 ।।

निहत्य तं मुनिश्रेष्ठ सुधन्वानं नराधिपम् ।
सांकाश्ये भ्रातरं शूरमभ्यषिञ्चं कुशध्वजम् ।। 19 ।।

कनीयानेष मे भ्राता अहं ज्येष्ठो महामुने ।
ददामि परमप्रीतो वध्वौ ते मुनिपुंगव ।। 20 ।।

सीतां रामाय भद्रं ते ऊर्मिलां लक्ष्मणाय च ।
वीर्यशुल्कां यम सुतां सीतां सुरसुतोपमाम् ।। 21 ।।

द्वितीयामूर्मिलांचैव त्रिर्वदामि न संशयः ।
ददामि परमप्रीतो वध्वौ ते रघुनन्दन ।। 22 ।।

रामलक्ष्मणयो राजन्गोदानं कारयस्व ह ।
पितृकार्यं च भद्रं ते ततो वैवाहिकं कुरु।। 23 ।।

मघा ह्यद्य महाबाहो तृतीये दिवसे प्रभो ।
फल्गुन्यामुत्तरे राजंस्तास्मिन्वैवाहिकं कुरु ।
रामलक्ष्मणयोरर्थे दानं कार्यं सुखोदयम् ।। 24 ।।
एवं भवतु भद्रं वः कुशध्वजसुते इमे ।
पत्न्यौ भजेतां सहितौ शत्रुघ्नमरतावुभौ ।। 25 ।।

Canto XIV (Canto LXXII of the present *Rāmāyaṇa*)

स गत्वा निलयं राजा श्राद्धं कृत्वा विधानतः
प्रभाते काल्यमुत्थाय चक्रे गोदानभुन्तमम् ।। 1 ।।

गवां शतसहस्राणि ब्राह्मणेभ्यो नराधिपः ।
एकैकशो ददौ राजा पुत्रानुद्दिश्य धर्मतः ।। 2 ।।

सुवर्णश्रृंगाः सम्पन्नाः सवत्साः कांस्यदोहनाः ।
गवां शतसहस्राणि चत्वारि पुरुषर्षभः ।। 3 ।।

वित्तमन्यच्च सुबहु द्विजेभ्यो रघुनन्दनः ।
ददौ गोदानमुद्दिश्य पुत्राणां पुत्रवत्सलः ।। 4 ।।

स सुतैः कृतगोदानैर्वृतश्च नृपतिस्तदा ।
लोकपालैरिवाभाति वृत्तः सौम्यः प्रजापतिः ।। 5 ।।

यस्मिंस्तु दिवसे राजा चक्रे गोदानमुत्तमम् ।
तस्मिंस्तु दिवसे शूरो युधाजित्समुपेयिवान् ।। 6 ।।

पुत्रः केकयराजस्य साक्षाद्भरतमातुलः ।
दृष्ट्वा पृष्ट्वा च कुशलं राजानमिदमब्रवीत् ।। 7 ।।

केकयाधिपती राजा स्नेहात्कुशलमब्रबीत् ।
येषां कुशलकामोऽसि तेषां संप्रत्यनामयम् ।। 8 ।।

स्वस्त्रीयं मम राजेन्द्र द्रष्टुकामो महीपते ।
तदर्थमुपयातोऽहमयोध्यां रघुनन्दन ।। 9 ।।

श्रुत्वा त्वहमयोध्यायां विवाहार्थं तवात्मजान् ।
मिथिलामुपयातांस्तु त्वया सह महीपते ।
त्वरयाभ्युपयातोऽहं द्रष्टुकामः स्वसुःसुतम् ।। 10 ।।

अथ राजा दशरथः प्रियातिथिमुपस्थितम् ।
दृष्ट्वा परमसत्कारैः पूजार्हं समपूजयत् ।। 11 ।।

ततस्तामुषितो रात्रिं सह पुत्रैर्महात्मभिः ।
ऋषींस्तदा पुरस्कृत्य यज्ञवाटमुपागमत् ।। 12 ।।

युक्ते मुहूर्ते विजये सर्वाभरणभूषितैः ।
भ्रातृभिः सहितो रामः कृतकौतुकमंगलः ।। 13 ।।

वसिष्ठं पुरतः कृत्वा महर्षीनपरानपि ।
पितुः समीपमाश्रित्य तस्थौ भ्रातृभिरावृतः ।। 14 ।।

वसिष्ठो भगवानेत्य वैदेहमिदमब्रवीत् ।
राजा दशरथो राजन् कृतकौतुकमंगलैः ।
पुत्रैर्नवरश्रेष्ठ दातारमभिकांक्षते ।। 15 ।।

दातृप्रतिगृहीतृभ्यां सर्वार्थाः प्रभवन्ति हि ।
स्वधर्मं प्रतिपद्यस्व कृत्वा वैवाह्यमुत्तमम् ।। 16 ।।

इत्युक्तः परमोदारो वसिष्ठेन महात्मना ।
प्रत्युवाच महातेजा वाक्यं परमधर्मवित् ।। 17 ।।

कः स्थितः प्रतिहारो मे कस्याज्ञा संप्रतीक्ष्यते ।
स्वगृहे को विचारोऽस्ति यथा राज्यमिदं तव ।। 18 ।।

कृतकौतुकसर्वस्वा वेदिमूलमुपागताः ।
मम कन्या मुनिश्रेष्ठ दीप्ता वह्नेरिवार्चिषः ।। 19 ।।

सज्जोऽस्मि त्वत्प्रतीक्षोऽस्मि वेद्यामस्यां प्रतिष्ठितः ।
अविघ्नं क्रियतां सर्वं किमर्थं हि विलम्ब्यते ।। 20 ।।

तद्वाक्यं जनकेनोक्तं श्रुत्वा दशरथस्तदा ।
प्रवेशयामास सुतान् सर्वानृषिगणानपि ।। 21 ।।

अब्रवीज्जनको राजा कौसल्यानन्दवर्धनम् ।
इयं सीता मम सुता सहधर्मचरी तव ।
प्रतीच्छ चैनां भद्रं ते पाणिं गृहणीष्व पाणिना ।। 22 ।।

लक्ष्मणागच्छ भद्रं ते ऊर्मिलामुद्यतां मया ।
प्रतीच्छ पाणिं गृह्णीष्व मा भूत्कालस्य पर्ययः ।। 23 ।।

तमेवमुक्त्वा जनको भरतं चाभ्यभाषत ।
गृहाण पाणिं पाण्डव्याः पाणिना रघुनन्दन ।। 24 ।।

शत्रुघ्नं चापि धर्मात्मा अब्रवीज्जनकेश्वरः ।
श्रुतकीर्त्या महाबाहो पाणिं गुह्णीष्व पाणिना ।। 25 ।।

सर्वे भवन्तः सौम्याश्च सर्वे सुचरितव्रताः ।
पत्नीभिः सन्तु काकुत्स्था मा भूत्कालस्य पर्ययः ।। 26 ।।

ज़नकस्य वचः श्रुत्वा पाणीन्पाणिभिरस्पृशन् ।
चत्वारस्ते चतुसृणां वसिष्ठस्य मते स्थिताः ।। 27 ।।

अग्निं प्रदक्षिणं कृत्वा वेदिं राजानमेव च ।
ऋषींश्चैव महात्मानः सहभार्या रघूत्तमाः ।
यथोक्तेन तथा चक्रुर्विवाहं विधिपूर्वकम् ।। 28 ।।

पुष्पवृष्टिर्महत्यासीदन्तरिक्षात् सुभास्वरा ।
दिव्यदुन्दुभिनिर्घोषै र्गीतवादित्रनिस्वनैः ।। 29 ।।

ननृतुश्चाप्सरःसंघा गन्धर्वाश्च जगुः कलम् ।
विवाहे रघुमुख्यानां तदद्भुतमिवाभवत् ।। 30 ।।

ईदृशे वर्तमाने तु तूर्योद्धुष्टनिनादिते ।
त्रिरग्निं ते परिक्रम्य ऊहुर्भार्या महौजसः ।। 31 ।।

अथोपकार्यां जग्मुस्ते सदारा रघुनन्दनाः ।
राजाप्यनुययौ पश्यन् सर्षिसंघः सबान्धवः ।। 32 ।।

Canto XV (Canto LXXVI of the present *Rāmāyaṇa*)

अथ राजा विदेहानां ददौ कन्याधनं बहु ।
गवां शतसहस्राणि बहूनि मिथिलेश्वरः ।। 1 ।।

कम्बलानां च मुख्यानां क्षौमकोटच्यम्बराणि च ।
हस्त्यश्वरथपादातं दिव्यरूपं स्वलंकृतम् ।। 2 ।।

ददौ कन्यापिता तासां दासीदासमनुत्तमम् ।
हिरण्यस्य सुवर्णस्य मुक्तानां विद्रुमस्य च ।। 3 ।।

ददौ परमसंहृष्टः कन्याधनमनुत्तमम् ।
दत्त्वा बहुधनं राजा समनुज्ञाय पार्थिवम् ।
प्रविवेश स्वनिलयं मिथिलां मिथलेश्वरः ।। 4 ।।

राजाप्ययोध्यापतिः सह पुत्रैर्महात्मभिः ।
चोदयामास तां सेनां जगामाशु ततः पुरीम् ।। 5 ।।

पताकाध्वजिनीं रम्यां तूर्योद्धुष्टनिनादिताम् ।
सिक्तराजपथां रम्यां प्रकीर्णकुसुमोत्कराम् ।। 6 ।।

राजप्रवेशसुमुखैः पौरैर्मंगलवादिभिः ।
संपूर्णां प्राविशद्राजा जनौधैः समलंकृताम् ।। 7 ।।

कृतदाराः कृतास्त्राश्च सधनाः ससुहृज्जनाः ।
शुश्रूषमाणाः पितरं वर्तयन्ति नरर्षभाः ।। 8 ।।

तेषाभतियशा लोके रामः सत्यपराक्रमः ।
स्वयंभूरिव भूतानां बभूव गुणवत्तरः ।। 9 ।।

रामस्तु सीतया सार्धं विजहार बहूनृतून् ।
मनस्वी तद्गतस्तस्या नित्यं हृदि समर्पितः ।। 10 ।।

प्रिया तु सीता रामस्य दाराः पितृकृता इति ।
गुणाद्रूपगुणाच्चापि प्रीतिर्भूयो व्यवर्धत ।। 11 ।।

तस्याश्च भर्ता द्विगुणं हृदये परिवर्तते ।
अन्तर्जातमपि व्यक्तमाख्याति हृदयं हृदा ।। 12 ।।

तस्य भूयो विशेषेण मैथिली जनकात्मजा ।
देवताभिः समा रूपे सीता श्रीरिव रूपिणी ।। 13 ।।

तचास राजर्षिसुतोऽभिरामया समेयिवानुत्तम राजकन्यया ।
अतीवरामःशुशुभेऽतिकामयाविभुःश्रियाविष्णुरिवामरेश्वरः ।। 14 ।।

Glossary

Ādikāvya	the first poem in classical Sanskrit, i.e., the Rāmāyaṇa of Vālmiki
akṛtadāra	one not having a wife
aṣṭāśīti	eighty-eight
aṣṭāviṁśati	twenty-eight
asura	demon
avatāra	incarnation of God
āyātena Sudūrāt	having come from afar
Caitra	the first month of Hindu calendar
caru	barley and pulse boiled for presentation to the gods and manes
caturviṁśat	twenty-four
catvāriṁśat	forty
dānava	demon
daitya	demon
etāni	these
Hallīśa dance	a kind of group dance
gadya kāvya	a poem composed in prose
*garuḍa*s	eagles
gotra	family descended from a particular *ṛṣi*
itihāsa	history

kāṇḍa	a section of a book
kāvya	poem
*mantra*s	prayers
nirvāṇa	death (literally emancipation)
pāyasa	rice boiled in milk
padya	verse
paraśu	axe
purāṇam ākhyānam	old narrative
purohita	domestic priest
putreṣṭi sacrifice	a sacrifice performed for obtaining a son
rājakṛt	king maker
rājasūya sacrifice	a kind of sacrifice performed by ancient Hindu kings
rākṣasa	name of a non-Aryan tribe of ancient India
rāsa dance	a kind of group dance
*ṛk*s	verses of the *Ṛgveda*
ṛṣabha	bull (this word figuratively means an eminent person)
ṛṣi	seer
ṛtu	season
*sāman*s	the chants of *Sāmaveda*
Śabar tribe	a non-Aryan tribe of south India
ṣaḍviṁśati	twenty-six
ṣaṇṇavati	ninety-six
ṣaṭtriṁśat	thirty-six
śloka metre	a metre of four lines with eight syllables

	in each line
Smṛtis	ancient Hindu law books
*suparṇa*s	see *garuḍa*s
*sūta*s	bards
tapas	austerity
triṁśat	thrity
upanayana ceremony	investiture of a Hindu boy with the sacred thread at the time of sending him for the study of the Vedas
Vānara	a non-Aryan tribe of south India
viṁśat	twenty
viṁśati	twenty
*yaju*s	prayers of the *Yajurveda*

Bibliography

VEDIC LITERATURE

Atharvaveda

Ṛgveda

Yajurveda — Kāṭhaka Saṁhitā

Yajurveda — Maitrāyaṇī Saṁhitā

Yajurveda — Taittirīya Saṁhitā

Yajurveda — Vājasaneyī Saṁhitā

Aitareya Brāhmaṇa

Jaiminīya Brāhmaṇa (including the *Jaiminīya Upaniṣad Brāhmaṇa*)

Pañcaviṁśa Brāhmaṇa

Sāmavidhāna Brāhmaṇa

Śatapatha Brāhmaṇa

Taittirīya Brāhmaṇa

Taittirīya Āraṇyaka

Bṛhadāraṇyaka Upaniṣad

Chāndogya Upaniṣad

Kauṣītaki Upaniṣad

VEDĀṄGA LITERATURE

Taittirīya Prātiśākhya

Baudhāyana Śrauta Sūtra

Śāṅkhāyana Śrauta Sūtra

Pāṇini's *Aṣṭādhyāyī*

PURĀṆAS

Agni Purāṇa

Bhāgavata Purāṇa

Brahma Purāṇa

Brahmāṇḍa Purāṇa

Brahmavaivarta Purāṇa

Garuḍa Purāṇa

Kūrma Purāṇa

Liṅga Purāṇa

Mārkaṇḍeya Purāṇa

Matsya Purāṇa

Padma Purāṇa

Skanda Purāṇa

Vāyu Purāṇa

Viṣṇu Purāṇa

EPICS

Rāmāyaṇa

Mahābhārata (including the *Bhagavad Gītā*)

Harivaṁśa

OTHER ANCIENT AND MEDIAEVAL HINDU WORKS

Adhyātma Rāmāyaṇa

Bhāsa — *Abhiṣeka*

Bhāsa — *Bālacarita*

Bhāsa — *Pratijñayaugandharāyaṇa*

Bhāsa — *Pratimā*

Bhāsa — *Svapnavāsavadattam*

Kālidāsa — *Abhijñāna-Śakuntalam*

Kālidāsa — *Raghuvaṁśa*

Kauṭilya — *Arthaśāstra*

Manu-smṛti

Patañjali — *Mahābhāṣya*

Śūdraka — *Mṛcchakaṭika*

BUDDHIST WORKS

Aśvaghoṣa-Buddhacarita

Dasaratha Jātaka

Dīgha Nikāya

Dīpavaṁsa — edited and translated by Oldenberg

Divyāvadāna

Ghaṭa Jātaka

Mahāvaṁsa — edited and translated by Geiger

Mahāvaṁsa ṭīkā — translated by Turnour

Majjhima Nikāya

JAIN WORKS

Hemacandra — *Pariśiṣṭaparavan*

Uttarādhyayana Sūtra

ANCIENT AND MEDIAEVAL FOREIGN ACCOUNTS OF INDIA

McCrindle — *Ancient India: Megasthenes and Arrian*

Sachau, E. — *Alberuni's India*

MODERN WORKS

Bhargava, P. L. : *India in the Vedic Age.*

———: *Vedic Religion and Culture.*

Bulke, C.: *Rāmakathā (Utpatti aur vikāsa)* (Hindi).

Jacobi, H. : *Das Rāmāyaṇa* (translated by S.N. Gohsal).

Keith, A. B. : *The Sanskrit Drama.*

Macdonell, A. A. : *A History of Sanskrit Literature.*

———: Keith, A. B.: Vedic Index of Names and Subjects.

Majumdar, R.C. and Pusalkar, A.D. : *The Vedic Age.*

Pargiter, F. E. : *Ancient Indian Historical Tradition.*

———: *Dynasties of the Kali Age.*

Pusalkar, A.D. : *Studies in the Epics and Purāṇas.*

Rapson, E. J. : *The Cambridge History of the India*, vol. I.

Raychaudhuri, H. C. : *Early History of the Vaiṣṇava Sect.*

———: *Political History of Ancient India.*

Winternitz, M. : *History of Indian Literature,* vol. I.

ARTICLES AND LECTURES

Bhargava, P. L. "On the Historicity of Rāma", *Srivenkatewara University Journal,* Golden Jubilee Volume, Tirupati 1989-91.

———: "A Fresh Appraisal of the Historicity of Indian Epics", *Annals of the Bhandarkar Oriental Research Institute, Poona,* Vol. LXIII, 1982.

Sircar, D.C.: "Rājavaṁśa varṇana of the Purāṇas", *Sir Venkatesvara University Oriental Journal,* Vol XX, Parts 1 and 2, 1977.

———:"Problems of the Rāmāyaṇa", Hyderabad, 1979.

Index

Abhijñāna-Śākuntalam, 38
Ābhīras, (Ahira), 64
Acyuta, 58
Adhisīmakṛṣna, 87
Adhvaryu, 35
Adhyātma Rāmāyaṇa, 93-97
ādikāvya, 93
Agni (God), 94
Agni Purāṇa, 10, 20, 27, 37, 43-45, 50, 56, 65, 66, 89, 90
Aihole inscription, 69
Aitareya Brāhmaṇa, 17, 35, 37, 46
Aja, 10
Ajaka, 72
Ajamīḍha, 4
Ajātaśatru, 5, 73-75, 77-79
  accession date, 79
Ajjaka, 72
akṛtadāra, 13, 14, 17
Akrūra 58, 60, 61
Alberuni, 90
Aṁśumat, 50
Ānakadundubhi, 57
Ancient Indian Historical Tradition, 95
ancient sages, 93
Andhakas, 57
Andhras, 2, 3, 6
Aniruddha, 63
Anu, 4
Apnavāna, 41
Araṇyakāṇḍa, 9, 16
archaeological excavation, 81
Ariṣṭa, 58
Arjuna, 61, 63, 64
Arjuna Sahasrabāhu, 42
Āryabhaṭa, 69
Āryaka, 72, 77, 79
Aryans, 1, 7
Aryans advent date, 7
Aryans arrival in India, 81
Aryans prophet, 35
Aśoka-grove, 18, 19
Assam, 61
Aṣṭādhyāyī, 55
aṣṭāśīti, 3
aṣṭāviṁśati, 3
asura, 7
Aśvaghoṣa, 97
  Buddhacarita
Atharvaveda, 86
  Sāmans, *Yajus*
Ātreya, 97
Atri, 97
Avantī, 2, 71-74
Avantīkhaṇḍa, 94
Avantivardhana, 72, 77, 79
Āvikṣita, 4

Ayāsya, 35
Ayodhyā, 14-17, 26, 28, 99
  royal families of, 16
Ayodhyākāṇḍa, 9, 10, 17, 94
Āyu, 4

Bāhu, 6, 45
Bālakāṇḍa, 9, 11, 17, 18
Balarāma, 8, 57-61, 65
Balbūtha, 7
Bālin, 8, 32, 34
  death of, 31
Bāṇa, 72
  Harṣacarita
barbarians, 17
bards, 86
  see also *sūtas*
Baudhāyana Śrauta Sūtra, 98
Besnagar, 55
Bhagavad Gītā, 38, 55, 63
Bhāgavata Purāṇa, 10, 20, 27, 37, 38, 43-45, 49-52, 56, 65, 66, 89, 90
Bhāgīratha, 8, 49-54
  austerities of, 50, 52
Bhāgīrathī, 49, 50
  see also Gaṅgā
Bharata, 4, 10, 13-16, 20, 26, 31, 37, 39, 49, 90
Bharata Dauḥṣanti, 4
Bharata *ṛṣabha*, 37
Bhārata War, 5, 63, 69, 80, 81
  date of , 81
Bhārgavas, 41
  ṛṣis of, 41
    Apnavāna, Bhṛgu, Cyavana, Dadhīca
Bhāsa, 2, 27, 74
  Svapnavāsavadattam
Bhaviṣya Purāṇa, 89, 90
Bhīma, 61
Bhīṣma, 46
Bhīsmaka, 59
Bhṛgu, 41, 96-98
Bhṛmyaśva, 4
Bihar, 2
Bimbisāra, 2, 71, 73-75, 77, 79
Brahmā (God), 67
Brahmakhaṇḍa, 67
Brahma Purāṇa, 10, 17, 18, 20, 27, 31, 35, 37, 44, 45, 50, 52, 53, 56, 65, 66, 89, 90
Brāhmaṇa, 88
Brāhmaṇas, 5, 56, 88, 94
Brahmāṇḍa Purāṇa 19, 20, 26-28, 37, 43, 45, 50, 51, 53, 56, 65, 66, 75, 86, 89, 90
Brahmavaivarta Purāṇa, 56, 66, 89, 90
  four sections, 67
    Brahmakhaṇḍa, Gaṇapati khaṇḍa, Prakṛtikhaṇḍa, Śrī Kṛṣna Janma-khaṇḍa
Bṛhadratha, 80
  invaluable information of, 80
Buddha, 2, 3, 70, 71, 78, 99
  Cantonese date, 78, date of birth, 78, era, 70, date of *nirvāṇa*, 78, 80, Sri Lankan date, 78
Buddhacarita, 97
Buddhism, 1, 99
Buddhist, 99
Buddhist accounts, 2
Buddhist Chronicles, 74
Buddhist traditions, 78
Buddhist *Ghaṭa Jātaka,* 55

Canton, 78
Cantonese date, 78
Cantonese reckoning, 78

Cāṇūra, 59
Cantos, 10-14, 16-20, 31-33, 94, 99
  spuriousness, 12
Caru, 42
Caturviṁśat, 3
Catvāriṁśat, 3
Cedi, 59, 62
Chāndogya Upaniṣad, 55
Chandragupta Maurya, 5, 55, 69-71, 79, accession of- 79, 80, Coronation of- 69, 70
Christian era, 7, 55
Citraratha, 43
Cola, 100
Cosmological chronology, 7
Cumuri, 8
Cyavana, 41, 96-98

Dadhīca, 41
daitya or *dānava*, 7
Dāmodara, 58
Dantavakra, 62
Darśaka, 2, 74, 75, 77, 79
Daśaratha, 2, 10-12, 14, 26, 41
Daśaratha Jātaka, 25
description of battle beatween Rāma & Bālin, 72
Devaka, 57
Devakī, 55, 57, 55, 65
Devarāta, 36
Dhṛtarāṣṭra Vaicitravīrya, 4, 5
Dhuni, 8
Dilipa, 50, 52
Dionysus, 5
Divyāvadāna, 74
Druhyu, 4, 52
Duryodhana, 60, 63
Duṣyanta, 37
Dvārakā, 59-64
  archaeological evidence, 81
Dynasties of the Kali Age, 2, 70

epic literature, 5
Eudemos, 79

fratricidal strife, 63

Gādhi, 36, 41, 97
Gaṇapatikhaṇḍa, 67
Gāndhāra, 52, 53
Gandharvas, 43
Gaṅgā, 49, 50
Garga, 58
Garuḍa Pruāṇa, 10, 17, 18, 20, 27, 28, 37, 50, 56, 65, 66, 89, 90
Gāthin, 36, 41, 97
Gautamī māhātmya, 27
Gāyatrī, 35
Ghaṭa Jātaka, 55
Ghora Āngirasa, 55
Ghosundi, 55
Girivraja, 74
Gokula, 57, 58, 66
Gomal (river) 53
Gomti (river) 53
Govinda, 58
Great Decease, 78
  dotter record of, 78
Greek gods, 5
  Dionysus
  Herakles
Gṛtsamada, 93, 94
Gujarat, 59, 81
Gupta dynasty 1

Haihayas, 43 45, 57
Haihaya Sahasrabāhu, 41
Hanumat,18-20, 28, 31

Hariścandra, 11, 17, 35, 36, 39, 46 49
Harivaṁśa, 10, 17, 18, 20, 25-28, 31, 37, 42-45, 50, 52, 53, 56, 65, 66
Harṣacarita, 72
Haryaṅka dynasty, 80
Hastināpura, 63, 69
hemistichs, 72, 74, 76
Herakles, 5, 55
Hinduism, 55
Hotṛ, 35
Hṛṣīkeśa, 58

Ikṣvākus, 4, 6, 26, 36, 42, 43, 45, 46, 49, 53, 54
Ikṣvāku Hariścandra, 41
Indo-Āryan History, 8
Indologists, 7, 97
Indra, 9, 10, 32, 38, 94
Indraprastha, 64
Indus (river), 53

Jacobi, 9-11, 13-18, 20, 25, 28, 99, 100
  his arguments, 98-99
Jāhnavī, 36, 54
Jahnu, 36, 54
  ancestors, 37,
  genealogy, 44
Jaiminīya Upaniṣad Brāhmaṇa, 49, 59
Jain accounts, 2
Jain Uharādhyayana Sūtra, 55
Jain tradition, 78
Jainism, 99
Jamadagni, 17, 35, 41-43, 46
  association of, 44
Jāmbavat, 60
Jāmbavatī, 60, 63
Janaka, 10-12
Janamejaya Pārikṣita, 5
Janasthāna, 26
Jarāsandha, 59, 61
Jaya, 90

Kākavarṇa, 9, 73
Kākavarṇa Saiśunāgī, 77
Kākavarṇa reign period, 78
Kākavarṇin, 74
Kālidāsa, 27, 38, 96
  Abhijñāna-Śākuntalam
  Raghuvaṁśa
Kaṁsa, 57-59
Kannauj, 36
Kaṇva, 38
Kaṇvas, 2
Kāṇvāyana, 71
Kānyakubja, 36, 41
  see also Kannauj
Kapila, 50, 93
Karma, 50
Kārtavīrya, 43-45
  his slaying, 43
Karusa, 62
Kāśī, 5, 74
Kauravas, 90
Kauśika, 37, 39
Kauśika *gotra*, 11
Kauṭilya, 86
  on *sūtras*, 86-87
Kekaya, 14, 16
Kerala, 100
Keśava, 58
Keśin, 58
Keśinisūdana, 58
Kirātas, 94
Kiṣkindhā, 32
Kiṣkindhākāṇḍa, 9, 31-33
Kliesobra (Kṛṣṇapura), 55

Kosala, 2, 27, 53, 54, 99
Kṛṣṇa, 5, 5, 41, 55-66, 97
fourteen works about, 56; intoduction of Rādhā, 66; lifting of Govardhan, 65; marriage with 16100 maidan, 64; marriage with Rādhā, 670; perfomance of *rāsa* dance, reconciliation efforts, 63; seizing of clothes, 66; sermons to Arjuna, 63; seventh sun, 65; taming of serpent Kāliya 65; worthiest guest, 62.
Kṛṣṇapura, 55
Kṛtavīrya, 42, 43
Kṣatraujas, 73, 77, 79, reign period, 74
Kṣemadharmajas, 72, 77
chronology 79
reign period, 76-77
Kṣemadharma, 73-75, 77
reign period, 75
Kṣemadharmatah, 74
Kṣemajit, 73
Kṣemavarman, 73
Kūrma Purāṇa, 10, 11, 17, 18, 20, 27, 28, 44, 45, 50, 56, 65, 66, 89, 90
Kuru, 5
Kurukṣetra, 63
Kuru-Pañcālas, 54
Kuśa, 18, 26
Kuśika, 36, 37, 97
Kuvalayāpīḍa, 58

Lakṣmaṇa, 8, 10, 11, 13, 15-18, 26, 33
Lakṣmī, 67
Laṅkā, 19-20,
burning of-18-20
Lava, 18, 26
Liṅga Purāṇa, 44, 45, 50, 56, 65, 66, 89, 90
Literature, 1
Buddhist, 1
Jain, 1
Lomaharṣana, 87-89
lunar race, 7

Macdonell, 99
Mādhava, 58
Madhu, 58
Magadha, 2, 59, 61, 71, 72, 74, 77, 80
Magadhan dynasty, 2
Mahābhārata, 8-10, 20, 25-28, 37, 38, 42, 43, 45, 46, 49-53, 56, 57, 63, 66, 81, 85, 90, 93, 94, 96
Mahābhāṣya, 55
Mahānandin, 6, 74, 77, 79
reign period, 75
Mahāpadma, 6, 69, 77
reign period, 77-78
Mahāvaṁśa, 70
Mahāvīra, 78
passing away date, 78
Majjhima Nikāya, 73
Mālinī (river), 38
Māndhātṛ, 4, 52, 53
Māndhātṛ Yauvanāśva, 4, 49
Mantharā, 15
Manu, 5,7
Vaivastva, 57
Mārkaṇḍeya Purāṇa, 89, 90
Marutta, 4
Mathurā, 55, 57-59
Matsya Purāṇa, 3, 26, 44, 45, 50, 56, 65, 66, 71, 74, 75, 89, 90, 96, 97
JMatsya, 75, *nMatsya*, 75, penultimate verse, 80
Mauryan empire, 79
Mauryas, 2
Max Müller, 7, 75

Megasthenes, 5, 6, 55
Menakā, 38, 39
Methora (Mathura), 55
Mithilā, 12, 99,
royal families, 16
Mṛcchakaṭikam, 72
Mura, 61
Muralīdhar, 58
Murāri, 61
Muṣṭika, 59

Nāgara Khaṇḍa, 94
Nāgārjunī hills, 2
Nahuṣa, 4, 41
Naimiṣa, 88
Nanaghat, 55
Nanda, 57, 58, 67, 76
Nandas, 2, 72
reign period, 78
Nandivardhana, 6, 72, 77, 79
reign period, 75, 77
Nārada Purāṇa, 89, 90
Naraka, 61, 64, 65
Niṣāda, 96
non-Aryan Association, 7
non-Aryan tribes, 7
numbers, 71
Caturviṁśat, Catvāriṁśat triṁśat, viṁśat

Padma Purāṇa, 9, 10, 20, 27, 43-45, 50, 56, 65, 66, 86, 89, 90, 97
Pālaka, 72, 74, 77, 79
Pañcāla, 5
Pāṇḍavas 60, 61, 63, 90
Pāṇḍya, 100
Pāṇini, 55
Aṣṭādhyāyī, 55
Panjāb, 79, 80
Paraśurāma, 8, 41-46, 93, 94
his adventure, 66, conflict with Kārtavīrya, 45, episode of discomfiture, 17, 18
Pargiter, F.E., 2, 70, 71, 75, 80, 95
Ancient Indian Historical Tradition
Dynasties of Kali Age
Parīkṣit II, 69
Pārvatī, 11
Pātāla Khaṇḍa, 66
Pāṭaliputra, 74, 99, 100
Patañjali, 55, 99
Mahābhāṣya, 55
Pauravas, 7
pāyasa, 12
Penultimate Verse, 80
Prabhāsa Khaṇḍa, 94
Pradyotas, 72-74, 77
account of 72-73
chronology, 79
Pradyumna, 63
Prāgyotiṣapura, 61, 64
Prākṛta, 72
Prakṛti Khaṇḍa, 67
Prasena, 59, 60
Prasenajit, 2
Pravāhaṇa Jaivali, 5
Pravarādhyāya, 98
Pulika, 72
Puṇḍra, 62
Puṇika, 72
Purāṇa Saṁhitā, 85-88, 90
Purāṇas, 1-9, 17, 18, 20, 26-28, 31, 36-39, 41-44, 49-53, 56, 57, 60, 64, 66, 67, 69, 70, 72, 73, 77-80, 85, 87, 90
chronology, 89
Cosmological account 7
earlier, 65

eighteen, 85
genealogical account, 25
later, 65
seven, 10
six, 20
text, 70-71
Purāṇic accounts,
chronology, 79, 90
evidence, 45
genealogical lists, 5
genealogies, 1, 3-6, 8, 69
list, 2-5, 70
literature, 5
studies, 1
Pūru, 4, 7
Purukutsa, 4, 49
Purūravas, 4, 37, 57
putraṣṭ sacrifice, 12

Rādhā, 56, 66
marriage with Kṛṣṇa, 67
mythical origin, 67
Raghuvaṁśa, 27
Rāhula, 2
rājasūya sacrifice, 35, 61
Rājavaṁśa Varṇana of the Purāṇas, 6
Rājagṛha, 73
rājkṛt, 86
rākṣasa, 7, 19
Rāma, 6, 8-12, 14-20, 25-29, 31-34, 39, 41, 46, 45, 56, 60, 93-96, 98, 99
account of - 26
association with Viśvāmitra, 18
banishment, 14, 15
coronation, 27
feat, 66
Journey to Mithila, 100
marriage 12-13
Rāma (prince), 41
Rāma (sage) 41
son of Jamadagni
Raṁa plays, 27
Rāmāyaṇa, 6, 8-10, 14-18, 20, 25, 26, 28, 31, 34, 49, 46, 56, 66, 93-95, 98, 99
composition, 99
designated as *ādikāvya*,
growth, 10
seven *kāṇḍas*, 9
Rāmopākhyāna, 20, 27
Rao, S.R., 81
Rapson, 72
Rāvaṇa, 12, 18, 19, 26
Ravikīrti, 69
Rāyaṇa, 67
Reychaudhuri, 3,
Political History of Ancient India
Ṛcīka, 41, 42
Reṇukā, 42-45
republican corporation, 63
Ṛgveda, 4, 5, 8, 25, 37, 38, 41, 51, 53, 57
poetic pieces, 35
Ṛgvedic age, 41, 46
Ṛkṣa, 97
Rohiṇī, 57, 65
Ṛṣyamūka hill, 32
Ṛṣyaśṛṅga, 12, 18
Ruci, 41
Rukmin, 59
Rukmiṇī, 59, 63

śabara tribe, 28
Ṣaḍviṁśati, 3
Sagara, 49, 50
Śaiva, 93
Śakas, 6

Sāketa, 99
Śakti, 67
Śakuntalā, 37-39
Śākya, 2
Śālva, 62
Sāmavidhāna Brāhamaṇa, 85
Sāmba, 63
Saṁhitās, 5, 25, 26,
Atharvaveda
Yajurveda
Sāndīpani, 59
Śambūka, 27, 28
Sandrakottos, 5
Sanghamukhya, 63
Saṅkarṣaṇa, 57, 58
Sāṅkhāyana Śrauta Sūtra, 37
Ṣaṇṇavati, 3
Sankrit literature, 1
language 93
Sarayū, 53
Śarmiṣṭhā, 7
Śaryāti, 41
Śatadhanvan, 60
Satiyaputra, 100
Satrājit, 59, 60
Śatrughna, 10,14, 16, 26
Śātvatas, 57, 63
Andhakas
Vṛṣnis
Satyabhāmā, 60, 65
Satyavatī, 41, 42
Sauhotṛ, 37
seizing of clothes of cowherdesses, 66
Siddhārtha, 2, 97
Sircar, D. C., 6-8
Rājavaṁśa Varṇana of the Purāṇas
Siritoi, 53
Śiśunāgas, 2, 3, 72-74,79
account of reign, 73-76, 78
Śiśunāgataḥ, 74
Śiśupāla, 59, 62
Sītā, 8, 10, 11, 13, 15, 16, 18-20. 26, 31,
abduction, 26
banishment, 8, 26, 28
coronation, 27,
crest jewel, 19, 20
exile, 27
Śiva, 11, 50, 52, 93, 94
Skanda Purāṇa, 11, 89, 90, 93-97
Śloka, 17
Smṛtis, 86
Sobhari Kāṇva, 53
Somaka, 4
Śravaṇaphala (reward), 27
Śrī Kṛṣṇa Janma Khaṇḍa, 67
Sri Lanka, 70, 74
Sri Lankan date, 78
tradition, 78
Sri Venkatesvara University Oriental Journal, 6
Subhadrā, 57, 61
Sudās, 35
Śuddhodana, 2, 97
Śūdra, 27
Sudyumna, 4, 57
Sugrīva, 31-33
Suhotra, 37
Sukalpa, 77
Sukanyā, 41
Sumitrā, 16
Śunaḥśepa, 35, 36
Sundarakāṇda, 9, 18
Śuṅgas, 2
Śunika, 72
Śūra, 97
Śurasena, 57
Śūrpaṇakhā, 13, 14, 17
Sūryaka, 72

sūtas, 16, 25, 86, 87
origin, 86
Vedic, 86
Suvāstu (river), 53
Svapnavāsavadattam, 2, 74
Swat, 53
Syamantaka, 59, 61, 65
Synchronism, 5
Syria, 81

Taittirīya Āraṇyaka, 85
Taittirīya Pratiśākhya, 98
tapas, 38, 50
Tārā, 32
Tarasadasyu Paurukutsi, 4
ten dynasties, 2
Andhras
Avanti
Kaṇvas
Kosala
Magadha
Mauryas
Nandas
Śiśunāgas
Śuṅgas
Vatsa
three great events, 69
three inscriptions, 55
Besanagar
Ghosundi
Nanaghat
Trasadasyu, 4, 49, 53
triṁśat, 3
Triśaṅku, 36
Tṛtsu, 4
dynasty 4
Sudās, 41
Tryaruṇa, 4
Turvaśa, 4

Udayana, 74
Udāyin, 74, 75, 77, 79, 99
Udgātṛ, 35
Ugarit, 81
Ugrasena, 57, 59, 63
Ugrasena Janaka, 5
Ujjain, 59
Upanayana ceremony, 59
Upaniṣads, 5, 88
Urmilā, 13, 16
Urva, 41
Uttarādhyayana Sūtra, 55
Uttarakāṇḍa, 9, 26-28, 66, 96

Vaidarbhas, 57
Vaiṣṇavakhaṇḍa, 94
Vaivasvata Manu, 7, 57
Mavantara, 7
Vajra, 64
Vālmīki, 8-10, 12, 13, 15-17 25- 27, 55, 93-100
Rāmāyaṇa
chain of evidence, 98
date of 98
composition of *Rāmāyaṇa*, 99
myths about, 94-95
story of early life, 96
Vāmana Purāṇa, 89, 90
Vānara, 18, 32, 33
Varāha Purāṇa, 89, 90
Vārāṇasī, 74
Vāraṇāvata, 60
Vārṣṇeya, 58
Vartivardhana, 72
Varuṇa (God), 35, 94
Vasiṣṭha, 13, 35, 36, 39, 41, 43, 85
Varudeva, 41, 55, 57-59, 62
Vatsa, 2, 74
Vatsapakṣa, 98

Vāyu Purāṇa, 3, 18, 20, 26-28, 37, 44, 45, 50-53, 56, 65, 66, 75, 77, 86, 89,
  text, 51
Vedas, 26, 87
Vedic age, 25, 35, 98
  Canon, 5
  literature, 9-5, 37-39, 49, 86
  Sanskrit, 98
  Works, 4
  Sāmavidhāna-Brāhmaṇa Taittirīya Āraṇyaka
Vidarbha, 59
Vidatha, 4
Videha, 5
Vidura, 63
Vikrama, 78
viṁśat, 3
Vindhyaśakti, 6
Virupākṣa, 20
Viśākhayūpa, 72, 77, 79
Viśālā, 99, 100
Viṣṇu (God), 45, 67, 94
Viṣṇu Purāṇa, 8-10, 18, 20, 28, 37, 44, 45, 50, 56, 65, 66, 86, 89, 90, 97
  condescension, 12
  incarnation, 18
Viśvāmitra, 8, 11-13, 18, 35-39 41, 42, 93, 94, 97
  austerities, 38
  conflict with Vasiṣṭha, 39
  Gāyatrī, 35
  lineage, 37
  magnanimaity, 36
  qualities, sacrifice, 35
Vṛndāvana, 55, 58, 66, 67
Vṛṣa parvan, 7
Vṛṣṇis, 57, 58
Vyāsa Pārāsarya, 8, 85-88, 90
  Purāṇa Saṁhitā, 85, 87

Waxhouse, 60
Winternitz, 7, 88, 99, 100
Worthiest quest, 62

Yādavas, 57
  branches
    Haihayas
    Sātvatas
    Vaidarbhas
Yadu, 4, 57
Yajurveda Saṁhitā, 86
Yama, 32
Yamunā, 57, 66
Yaśodā, 57, 67
Yavanas or Greeks, 6, 99
Yayāti, 4, 7
  Sons
    Anu Druhya
    Pūru
    Turvaśa
    Yadu
Yayāti Nāhuṣa, 4, 57
Yudhājit, 13, 14
Yuddhakāṇḍa, 8, 27, 28
Yudhiṣṭhira, 8, 61, 63, 69 Coronation, 9, 81
Yūpākṣa, 20